DANISH YEARBOOK
OF
PHILOSOPHY

VOLUME 38

DANISH YEARBOOK
OF
PHILOSOPHY

VOLUME 38
2003

MUSEUM TUSCULANUM PRESS
UNIVERSITY OF COPENHAGEN 2004

Published for
Dansk Filosofisk Selskab
in cooperation with
the Philosophical Societies of Aarhus and Odense
and with financial support from
the Danish Research Council for the Humanities

*

EDITORIAL BOARD:

FINN COLLIN
University of Copenhagen
Chairman

UFFE JUUL JENSEN
University of Aarhus

SVEN ERIK NORDENBO
University of Copenhagen

STIG ANDUR PEDERSEN
Roskilde University Centre

ERICH KLAWONN
Odense University

HANS SIGGAARD JENSEN
Copenhagen Business School

MOGENS PAHUUS
Aalborg University

*

Articles for consideration and all editorial communications should be sent in three copies to:
Danish Yearbook of Philosophy
University of Copenhagen, Department of Philosophy
Njalsgade 80, DK 2300 Copenhagen S, Denmark

Business communications, including subscriptions and orders for reprints, should be addressed to the publishers:
MUSEUM TUSCULANUM PRESS
Njalsgade 94
DK 2300 Copenhagen S
Denmark

*

© 2004 DANISH YEARBOOK OF PHILOSOPHY
COPENHAGEN, DENMARK
PRINTED IN DENMARK
BY SPECIAL-TRYKKERIET VIBORG

ISBN 87-7289-989-1
ISSN 0070-2749

CONTENTS

Morten Hansen: *The Theses of Identity in Z_6 and H_6 of Aristotle's Metaphysics* 7

Peter Wolsing: *Der Begriff der sittlichen Vernunft bei dem jungen Hegel* 37

Jesper Kallestrup: *Privileged Access and Two Kinds of Semantic Externalism* 57

Lars Binderup: *Quasirealism or Minimalism?* 65

Niels Thomassen: *The Ethics of Understanding* 83

Erich Klawonn: *The Metaethical Foundations of Human Rights* 99

Thomas Petersen: *Egalitarianism and Repugnant Conclusions* 115

THE THESES OF IDENTITY IN Z_6 AND H_6 OF ARISTOTLE'S *METAPHYSICS*

MORTEN HANSEN

Department of Philosophy
University of Southern Denmark

As long as Aristotle's *Metaphysics* has been read and interpreted, the question whether ousia is to be considered as universal or particular has been the subject of much debate and seems, admittedly, as puzzling today as ever. In this paper, which presents one of the cornerstones of my interpretation of Aristotle's metaphysics, I shall address this very problem in relation to Z_6 and H_6.

My main thesis is that Aristotle operates with a universal as well as a particular conception of ousia and that these have different functions and serve specific purposes in his theory and further that this duality is not necessarily damaging to the theory as a whole. Moreover this reading offers us the advantage of not having to explain away the fact that Aristotle's text actually provides us with numerous examples of both particular and universal ousiai. Hence, in this paper I Intend to demonstrate that such a metaphysical outlook is very productive to the interpretation of Z_6 as well as H_6 and even more importantly, that Z_6 and H_6 prove very productive to this overall interpretation.

I

The main topic of investigation in Z_6 is the following imperative:

"Πότερον δὲ ταὐτόν ἐστιν ἢ ἕτερον τὸ τί ἦν εἶναι καὶ ἕκαστον, σκεπτέον" 1031a 15-16

"Let us inquire whether what-being-is is identical with each-thing, or different."

This passage suggests an examination of whether what-being-is is identical with each-thing or not. Nevertheless, this is not the real enterprise of Z_6. If we read a little further another project reveals itself:

"Ἔστι γάρ τι πρὸ ἔργου πρὸς τὴν περὶ τῆς οὐσίας σκέψιν· ἕκαστόν τε γὰρ οὐκ ἄλλο δοκεῖ εἶναι τῆς ἑαυτοῦ οὐσίας, καὶ τὸ τί ἦν εἶναι λέγεται εἶναι ἡ ἑκάστου οὐσία." 1031a 16-18

> "This is useful for our inquiry about ousia, for each-thing is thought to be nothing else but its own ousia, and what-being-is is said to be the ousia of each-thing."

According to Aristotle, we do in fact believe that each-thing is identical with its ousia and further that what-being-is is ousia and consequently also identical with each-thing. Hence, the question is not whether there is identity or not, but why we actually believe this. This point will turn out to be of significance to the interpretation of Z_6.

However, in my interpretation I shall initially comment on the key concepts of Z_6 and try to answer the following questions: what is meant by each-thing (ἕκαστον)? what is meant by what-being-is (τὸ τί ἦν εἶναι)? and what is meant by identity (τὸ αὐτό)?

II

The ἕκαστον (each-thing) is not easily translated. Tredennick translates it into "the particular thing"[1], Bonitz translates into "jedes einzelne Ding"[2] and Tricot even translates into "chaque être".[3]

The most popular understanding of ἕκαστον is that it denotes 'the particular physical object' in some sense of the word. I am, however, not convinced of the appropriateness of this. First, if we were to read the ἕκαστον in this way and if Aristotle found that he had given a satisfactory account of the ousia of the particular compound, why then did he readdress the issue anew in H_6? Second, (as Frede/Patzig[4] have pointed out) if Aristotle were to denote the particular object, why did he not use τὸ καθ᾽ ἕκαστον which elsewhere is used as a technical expression denoting just this?

It is more likely that ἕκαστον is to be read in relation to its context. The inexact and unspecified 'each thing' or 'any thing' is to be read in relation to the overall question, namely the question of ousia. Hence, 'each thing' means 'each thing' of relevance, i.e. *'each thing which is itself an ousia'*. In this sense each-thing is not just any-thing but each-this which has or rather *is* its own ousia. Consequently, what the expression is meant to denote, is *the particular or individual ousia* which each-thing *is,* and the particular individual ousia is *the particular form or the particular what-being-is*. However, before the consequences of this interpretation are drawn, I shall deal with the concepts of what-being-is and identity.

III

The τὸ τί ἦν εἶναι is an obscure neologism of Aristotle's which has proved difficult to interpret. However, I believe some questions have been answered satisfactorily. As to the understanding of the Greek expression I find that especially Bassinge[5] has presented a plausible explanation. In the following I shall give a survey of how I believe the expression is best accounted for.

First, the expression is to be read in analogy to the so-called Aristotelian dative, i.e. expressions like τὸ ἀνθρώπῳ εἶναι ('to be human') and τὸ ἀγαθῷ εἶναι ('to be good'), etc.[6] i.e. the article (τὸ) substantivizes the infinitive (τὸ ... εἶναι) and the τί ἦν is understood as an insertion.

Second, the interrogative pronoun τί is, as Arpe[7] argues, to be read in analogy to the so-called Socratic question, namely the τί ἐστι? (what is it?).[8] At the time of Aristotle, Socrates' thinking is still vivid among philosophers. The Socratic τί ἐστι? asks '*what* is ...?' and this question is answered by a definition. But does the τί in τὸ τί ἦν εἶναι only ask for an essential definition of 'what' the thing is? In order to answer this question, I believe we must view the τί in connection with the imperfect ἦν as well as with the infinitive εἶναι.

The infinitive affects the τί in the sense that it, as Weidemann puts it, "befragt (...) nicht etwa eine *Sache* darauf hin, was *sie* ist, sondern es befragt das durch den Infinitiv εἶναι bezeichnete *Sein* einer Sache darauf hin, was *es* ist"[9] The function of the τί in the expression is not only to ask for a 'what' in the sense of a pure essence, but to ask for being. Hence, the τί in the infinitive leaves us with a semantic discrepancy between the 'what' and the 'being'. But before elaborating on this matter, I shall take a closer look at the ἦν, and further at τί ἦν.

The imperfect ἦν is the part of the expression which has caused most trouble to the interpreters. I believe a plausible account is given in the so-called philosophical imperfect. Ross[10] notes: "ἦν is said to be a *'philosophical imperfect'*,[11] referring to something stated earlier in the argument"[12] The use of an imperfect to refer to what is mentioned earlier is certainly to be found in Aristotle,[13] but if the 'philosophical imperfect' is to give a general account of the ἦν in the τὸ τί ἦν εἶναι, it must be possible to find a referent. However, a brief glance at the text reveals that this demand cannot be met and Ross consequently rejects this interpretation. Bassenge, on the other hand, finds support in Schwyzler's account of an 'attractio temporis', "Naturgegebene, geographische, ethnologische u.a. Tatbestände, die an keine Zeit gebunden sind oder doch von der Vergangenheit in die Gegenwart des Sprechenden hineinreichen, werden in der Erzählung gewönlich als vergangen gesehen, wenn sie mit einem Vorgang der Vergangenheit in Verbindung stehen"[14] The imperfect does not necessarily refer to an earlier stated present tense, it might instead refer to a non-temporal 'entity' which is understood and expressed in the past tense. However, we find nothing explicitly referred to, and the imperfect must be understood as a βραχυλογία (brevity in speech) or, as Bassenge puts it, as an 'elliptische attractio temporis'. Hence the philosophical imperfect is understood as an elliptic expression, but what is omitted? Bassenge's account "… erklärt das Imperfectum nicht daraus, daß es sich um eine *Sache* handelt, von der schon *die Rede war,* sondern daraus, daß es sich um ein *Sein* handelt, das sich jeweils als solches *erwiesen hatte.*"[15] The imperfect tense is used to announce being in its being, and in that sense it does not refer to something stated earlier, but to *the being of the being in question.*

Another plausible reading of the imperfect is *the imperfect of duration.* In Greek, aspect is used not only to separate the various tenses but also, and maybe primarily, to qualify types of action or rather the aspect in which the action is viewed.[16] Hence the imperfect expresses duration, and the translation of ἦν into 'was' is in that respect not an appropriate choice – a better alternative might be 'was, is, and will be'. The τί ἦν expresses what a thing permanently *is,* i.e. what *is* behind its genesis and destruction, its changing properties etc. Against the imperfect of duration Bassenge argues that it is linked to another interpretation, namely to the interpretation of the relation between form, matter, and compound (σύνολον).

> "φανερὸν ἄρα ὅτι οὐδέ τὸ εἶδος, ἢ ὁτιδήποτε χρὴ καλεῖν τὴν ἐν τῷ αἰσθητῷ μορφήν, οὐ γίγνεται, οὐδ' ἔστιν αὐτοῦ γένεσις, οὐδὲ τὸ τί ἦν εἶναι" 1033b 5-7
>
> "It is clear, then, that neither does the form, or whatever one should call the shape of a perceptible thing, itself come into being or undergo generation, nor does the what-being-is"

In accordance with a Platonic way of thinking, what does not come into being or undergo generation is believed to have eternal being. Following this premise, Aristotle says that form and what-being-is *are* eternal. As Ross points out in his commentary to this passage, this is not as self-evident a reading as it seems at first sight. "Aristotle does not necessarily mean that form is eternal. Sometimes he says that it comes into being and passes out of being instantaneously"[17] Actually, if Aristotle were to give 'eternal existence' to the what-being-is, he would evidently end in the very same Platonic kind of idealism which, I believe, all his efforts are put forward to avoid. Hence, what comes to be and ceases to be, and changes in between these, is the compound (σύνολον), but neither matter nor what-being-is nor form. However, this idea does not imply that what is not in generation and destruction has eternal existence or the like. In this respect I believe Bassenge is right in his philosophical argument against the interpretation of duration.

Nevertheless, another sense of duration is possible. The ἦν does not necessarily express an eternal thing, duration might instead be attached to the τί (what) of the thing. The ἦν is not isolated, it is a τί ἦν (*what* it was, is or will be). It is *what* the thing *is,* in so far as it is, but *what* the thing is, is not itself a thing, separate from the particular things. Hence, the duration is not a duration of existence of a thing, it is the duration of 'a what', and this 'what' could either (i) be understood as a kind of structure which the existing thing has in order to be, i.e. as a structural, ontological principle rather than as an existing thing of some sort. The structure does not in itself exist like a thing does, however, it *is* in some sense of the word – it is what the thing is in order to be. Further, (ii) the 'what' could be understood as a conceptual precondition for the experience of the particular compound, i.e. in an epistemological sense and in this sense the τί ἦν asks for an epistemological principle.

Hence, if we distinguish the different senses of duration, the imperfect of duration offers, as well as the philosophical imperfect, a plausible understanding of the ἦν. I find it hard to choose between these interpretations of the ἦν, as I believe a grain of truth is hidden in each of them. The first interpretation gives a very plausible account of a philosophical imperfect denoting a persistent being.[18] This interpretation presents what-being-is as *an ontological ἀρχή*[19] of the things which *are* (τὰ οὔτα). From a philosophical point of view, the philosophical imperfect is very similar to what I called the ontological duration. This too speaks of an ontological ἀρχή which is not thought of in terms of a thing, i.e. it does not exist like a thing or a Platonic idea. Both interpretations are ontological whereas the second interpretation of duration understands the ἦν as a conceptual ἀρχή or an epistemological principle.

To give a simplified account of the matter, if we stress the τί in τί ἦν, the consequence will be that the whole expression is understood as denoting a concept of some sort. On the other hand, if we stress the ἦν in τί ἦν, the whole expression will be thought of as denoting some sort of foundation of being (Seinsgrund). However, I believe that no textual evidence can be put forward to support either of these readings, at the expense of the other. Instead we ought to ask whether these two types of readings are in fact in conflict with each other.

One way of dealing with the issue is to look at it from a philosophical point of view. What kind of priority do the interpretations stress? The ἦν in the sense of epistemological principle is only possible if some conceptual 'what' is preconceived, and this 'what' *is* in some sense of the word. On the other hand, no abstract concept *is* in the strict sense of the word, it *is what* the thing is. Hence, no concept has an independent existence, but *expresses the independence of the thing that is*. Without some ὄντα, the epistemological concept of 'what the thing is' would be absurd. However, as Kahn[20] puts it, the thought of radical contingency does not appear in Aristotle's line of thinking, he never contemplates the possibility that nothing is. The existence of the world and the existence of an ordered world were never questions for philosophical inquiry in Aristotele's thinking; it was taken for granted. Consequently, concepts are never just epistemological concepts, they are concepts of something, namely of being or beings. The so-called epistemological concept of a 'what' really depends on something being 'what it is'. We can then establish an ontological order among the remaining interpretations of the imperfect.

We find the primary sense of the ἦν in Bassenge's understanding of the philosophical imperfect or the ontological durative. This poses a being which on the other hand is accessible from an epistemological point of view, in the sense that *'what* the thing is' is an epistemological precondition for knowing the thing at all; and this again is only possible if the concept of the thing in some sense of the word *is*.

As simile of Plato's divided line,[21] the issue can be viewed from an ontological as well as an epistemological point of view. Ontologically speaking, the philosophical imperfect is prior, then follows the epistemological durative. Epistemologically speaking, the reverse is the case.

Hence, from a philosophical point of view, we do not have to choose one interpretation at the expense of the others, and the whole expression could, as many others, be used at several levels, as e.g. οὐσία which means the concrete changeable form/matter thing, the unmoved mover, form, etc. and as e.g. ὑποκείμενον which means form/matter thing, form, and matter, etc. Hence, as a preliminary assumption we might understand the whole expression as both an ontological and epistemological concept.

Further, the τό makes it clear that the whole expression is supposed to be an answer, but what question is answered? If we ask, 'what is man?' Aristotle might have replied 'τὸ ἀνθρώπῳ εἶναι' ('what it is to be man'), but again one might ask, 'τί ἐστι τὸ ἀνθώπῳ εἶναι?' ('what is it to be man?'), the answer might be given with the definition 'τὸ δίπουν ζῷον' ('a biped animal'). In analogy to this one might ask, 'what is a thing?' (in the sense of anything or any being or everything). Aristotle might have answered, 'τὸ ἑκάστῳ εἶναι' ('what it is for everything to be'), and further, we might ask, 'τί ἐστι τὸ ἑκάστῳ εἶναι' ('what is it for everything to be?'). It is not in this case possible to give a specific definition of a kind or genus of being, since this is evidently not what is asked for. Instead one must answer by proposing a definition of a thing as such (i.e. with regard to its being), but again, this definition cannot be defined by setting a limit (ὅρος) between beings of different kinds (e.g. biped and not biped, etc.) since nothing literally falls outside the definition. Hence, 'τὸ τί ἦν εἶναι' is the answer,[22] it denotes being as such, not a kind of being. Nevertheless, in relation to the particular thing or the particular kind of thing, what-being-is is something specific, it is the definition of the thing, it is what is said of the thing in its own right (καθ' αὑτό).

It is a common feature in Aristotle's thinking that terms and concepts are used in various ways and they are always to be read in relation to a concrete discussion. This is the case with what-being-is as well. We might distinguish between three different levels of use of what-being-is. (i) In Δ_{18} we learned that Callias has his own what-being-is. In Z_4 'being you' is used as an example of what-being-is, which indicates that Aristotle to some degree and in some sense considers it possible and meaningful to speak of the particular what-being-is of the particular thing, this sense we might refer to as *particular-what-being-is*. (ii) In Z_8 we learned that neither form nor what-being-is undergoes generation, but only the compound. And further, that form (and we might insert what-being-is) contrary to what is said in Z_4 is not a-this but rather a such-a-kind (τὸ τοιόνδε). What-being-is is evidently here understood as the universal species, this we shall call *universal-what-being-is*. (iii) When discussed isolated from the particular things (τὰ ὄντα) what-being-is is not understood as the what-being-is of a particular thing or kind of thing but simply and plainly as Being[23] i.e. not in the sense of a being thing (τὸ ὄν in German 'das Seiende') but in the sense of Being (ὄν or οὐσία, in German 'Sein'). In this sense what-being-is only distinguishes between *being* and *not-bein* in a primary sense of the word, as it simply and plainly denotes Being. This sense of what-being-is I shall call *what-Being-is*.

Z_6 is to be read in relation to especially Z_4 and Z_5 and in order to give meaning to the identity posed in Z_6 we have to look briefly into Z_{4-5}. Aristotle intends as stated in the beginning of Z_4, to say something λογικῶς about the matter.[24] A key to the translation of λογικῶς is given later when it is stated that 'definition' (ὁρισμός) is used in several senses. Just like 'is' is used denoting both ousia and the other predicates, so is definition used, first to define ousia, and second to define the other predicates. However, the definition of secondary predicates cannot be stated without qualification (ἁπλῶς), as it presupposes something else. And Aristotle proceeds: "ἀλλ' ὥσπερ ἐπὶ τοῦ μὴ ὄντος λογικῶς φασί τινες εἶναι τὸ μὴ ὄν" 1030a 25-26 ("but just like in the case of what is not, some make the linguistic [or logical] point that what is not is." This passage shows that what is said λογικῶς[25] denotes some linguistic or logical point and not an ontological one. Hence, what we are to expect from the following, i.e. chapters 4 and 5 and chapter 6 is first of all a linguistic and logical analysis of what-being-is.

The only passage which refers to an particular-what-being-is is in the beginning of Z_4 where 'being you' (τὸ σοὶ εἶναι) is used in analogy to what-being-is as what is said of something in-its-own-right (καθ' αὑτό). There is no doubt, I think, that Aristotle here gives an example of what is meant by what-being-is. Hence, what is analysed in Z_{4-5} is the universal-what-being-is and the what-Being-is.

Moreover, these two senses are in fact merged in Aristotle's analysis. Z_{4-5} is the nearest we get to an analysis of what-being-is as such, i.e. in the sense of what-Being-is. And even here it is not considered independently but always in relation to the thing of which it is the what-being-is i.e. as universal-what-being-is.[26] Hence, without saying too much, the what-being-is claimed to be identical with 'each thing' in Z_6 is the universal-what-being-is which is the ontological and epistemological principle of things. This leaves us with the third key-concept to be dealt with, namely identity.

IV

The Greek word for identity or to use a more direct translation 'the same' is τὸ αὑτό. In book Δ of the *Metaphysics*[27] we find an account of the different senses of 'the same'. First 'the same' is said of what is coincidentally (κατὰ συμβεβηκός) the same, as e.g. 'man' and 'cultured' are the same if the thing denoted e.g. Socrates is in fact cultured. What makes 'cultured' and 'man' the same is in fact that a particular compound is actually a cultured man. This sense is of course of no relevance to Z_6 as what-being-is is not coincidentally predicated of the thing.

Next, 'the same' is used of what is in-its-own-right (καθ' αὐτό) 'the same' and 'one' and Aristotle proceeds "καὶ γὰρ ὧν ἡ ὕλη μία ἢ εἴδει ἢ ἀριθμῷ ταὐτὰ λέγεται, καὶ ὧν ἡ οὐσία μία"[28] ("for things whose matter is formally or numerically one and for things whose ousia is one are said to be the same") What is remarkable at first hand is that Aristotle distinguishes between formal and numerical identity and by this distinction he indicates that formal identity is something quite different from numerical identity. Nevertheless, this is only superficially true since matter is one (μία) either formally or numerically, i.e. the matter might be *one* formally (and thereby not numerically). But what is a non-numerical-one?

This question can only be answered if 'one' is applied to a broader ontological field as is the case with 'numerical identity'. I believe numerical identity is applicable to the particular existing thing or things, i.e. the canvas, the oar and the planks are numerically one thing, namely a boat, or the conglomerate of boats is one thing, namely a fleet, etc. However, the form or ousia is one, namely a principle, we might even say that it is principally one and therefore not numerical. Hence, in relation to the pure countability of the existing things Callias and Socrates are two things but in relation to *what* they are, namely 'a man' they are 'the same'[29]. If this account of 'being one' and 'being countable' is right, the passage is comprehensible and the next task is to apply this result to the concrete thesis of identity claimed in Z_6.

Given the results of the analysis of each-thing, what-being-is and identity we find that each-thing (in the sense of 'each thing' or 'any thing' – of relevance, i.e. 'each thing which is itself an ousia' i.e. particular form or particular what-being-is) is identical with or the-same as the universal-what-being-is. Hence, what Aristotle in fact tries in Z_6 is to unite the two strands in the *Metaphysics* which have caused the interpreters so much trouble, namely the particular and the universal. In the following I shall read the rest of Z_6 in the light of this understanding of the thesis of identity and see whether it fits the *Metaphysics*.

V

As Aristotle puts it in the second quotation[30] "each-thing is thought to be nothing else but its own ousia, and what-being-is is said to be the ousia of each-thing." In accordance with my interpretation this means that the universal-what-being-is which is the object of our knowledge and the ousia of each-thing i.e. its particular form or what-being-is are the-same. Nowhere in Z_6 does Aristotle in fact question the thesis; it is self-evident. But it is still interesting to follow Aristotle's reasoning on this issue.

As in Z_4 and Z_5, Aristotle distinguishes in Z_6 between what is said coincidentally (κατὰ συμβεβηκός) and what is said in-its-own-right (καθ' αὑτό). In Z_4 and Z_5 the conclusion was that what is spoken of coincidentally either has no what-being-is or has it in a derived sense. In Z_6 it is evidently a primary sense of what-being-is which is discussed, and it comes as no surprise to the reader that Aristotle does not consider what is spoken of coincidentally as identical with its what-being-is. Nevertheless, the arguments are of interest.

Aristotle presents two reductio ad absurdum arguments[31] (which shall be accounted for in outline.[32]) (i) If 'pale man' is identical with what-being-is for 'pale man', and 'pale man' is identical with man (and man is identical with what-being-is for man), then what-being-is for 'pale man' is identical with what-being-is for man, which is absurd. Therefore the initial assumption, that 'pale man' is identical with what-being-is for 'pale man', must be abandoned. (ii) If 'pale man' is identical with what-being-is for 'pale man', then what-being-is for 'pale man' is identical with what-being-is for 'man'. But if this is the case the same can be said about 'cultured'. If what-being-is for 'pale man' is identical with what-being-is for 'man', and if what-being-is for 'cultured man' is identical with what-being-is for 'man', then what-being-is for 'pale man' is identical with what-being-is for 'cultured man', and this is absurd too.

In one sense what-being-is for 'pale man' is identical with what-being-is for man, but it is only a coincidental identity,[33] and Aristotle is obviously not interested in what by chance is the same. Hence, we shall turn to what is spoken of in-its-own-right.

> "ἐπὶ δὲ τῶν καθ' αὑτὰ λεγομένων ἆρ' ἀνάγκη ταὐτὸ εἶναι, οἷον εἴ τινες εἰσὶν οὐσίαι ὧν ἕτεραι μὴ εἰσὶν οὐσίαι μηδὲ φύσεις ἕτεραι πρότεραι, οἵας φασὶ τὰς ἰδέας εἶναί τινες;"
> 1031a 28-31
>
> "regarding what is spoken of in-its-own-right, are they necessarily the same (as their what-being-is)? For instance, if there are some ousiai, which have no other ousiai or natures prior to them, just like the ideas are said to be ousiai"

What is discussed here is the question: if ousiai are true ousiai (i.e. are primary in being, and have no other ousia, or any other kind of being prior to them), are ousiai then identical with their what-being-is? From the examples used in the following argument (namely, αὐτὸ τὸ ἀγαθόν (goodness itself), and τὸ ὄν (being)), it is evident that Aristotle analyses ousia as a concept, since 'goodness' and 'being' have no what-being-is according to Aristotle himself – the examples are taken from Plato's philosophy. Thus, in this respect, it is irrelevant whether we confess to Plato's or Aristotle's metaphysical theories. As long as we operate with a philosophy of ousia, some consequences have to be drawn from it, namely that ousia is identical with its what-being-is.[34] Aristotle gives three main arguments for this which are connected in a complete line of reasoning:

> "εἰ γὰρ ἔσται ἕτερον αὐτὸ τὸ ἀγαθόν καὶ τὸ ἀγαθῷ εἶναι, καὶ ζῷον καὶ τὸ ζῴῳ, καὶ τὸ ὄντι καὶ τὸ ὄν, ἔσονται ἄλλαι τε οὐσίαι καὶ φύσεις καὶ ἰδέαι παρὰ τὰς λεγομένας, καὶ πρότεραι οὐσίαι ἐκεῖναι, εἰ τὸ τί ἦν εἶναι οὐσία ἐστίν." 1031a 31-b2
>
> "If then goodness itself is different from what it is to be good, animality is different from what it is to be an animal, and being is different from what it is to be, then there would be other ousiai, natures, and ideas in relation to those mentioned, and these will be prior, if what-being-is is ousia."

If what-being-is is ousia (i.e. primary), and if the ousiai are not identical with their what-being-is, then there will be other ousiai prior to the first ones, and this would be the true ousiai. A few lines further down[35] Aristotle tries to elucidate the point by giving names to each what-being-is. If what-being-is is not identical with ousia, we would then have to name yet another what-being-is for horse,[36] – and what to call this? The argument is taken even further:

> "οὐ γὰρ κατὰ συμβεβηκὸς ἓν τὸ ἑνὶ εἶναι καὶ ἕν. ἔτι εἰ ἄλλο ἔσται, εἰς ἄπειρον εἶσιν· τὸ μὲν γὰρ ἔσται τί ἦν εἶναι τοῦ ἑνὸς τὸ δὲ τὸ ἕν, ὥστε καί ἐπ᾽ ἐκείνων ὁ αὐτὸς ἔσται λόγος." 1032a 1-4
>
> "It is not coincidental that unity and what it is to be a unity are one, if they were different, we would have an infinite regress. On the one hand, we would have what-being-is of unity, on the other hand, unity. Hence, the same argument can be repeated for these too."

If ousia is not identical with its what-being-is, there will be yet another ousia. But this argument can be used of the second ousia as well, and then we have a third ousia, and so on. If we were to stop at the second or tenth ousia, the one we would stop at would be identical with its what-being-is. Hence, either we have an identity between ousia and its what-being-is or we have an infinite regress. This argument is followed by another argument.

"καὶ εἰ μὲν ἀπολελυμέναι ἀλλήλων [i.e. οὐσίαι, φύσεις, ἰδέαι and τὸ τί ἦν εἶναι], τῶν μὲν οὐκ ἔσται ἐπιστήμη τὰ δ' οὐκ ἔσται ὄντα" 1031b 3-4

"And if the two are divorced from one another, then ousia will be unknowable, and what-being-is will have no being"

According to both Plato and Aristotle, knowledge of the thing is knowledge of *what the thing is,* and in this connection it means that knowledge of ousia is knowledge of its what-being-is.[37] If ousia and what-being-is were different, we would have no knowledge of ousia at all, since it would be of the form 'A is B', and when we want to know B, the answer might then be 'B is C', etc. This either stops, and we might ask 'what is S, P, or Q?' and they have to be identical with their what-being-is, or it does not stop, and we will never have knowledge of any being. Further, there is an additional but very important conclusion. Not only would we have no knowledge of ousia if ousia were not identical with its what-being-is, but what-being-is would have no being. Hence, if we were to have any knowledge, it would not be of anything (i.e. any being), and if there were anything at all, it would be principally unknowable, since no what-being-is would *be*. This second conclusion will help us to grasp what the identity is all about.

VI

The thesis of identity can of course be seen as an answer to Plato's alleged problem of self-predication.[38] If 'goodness itself' is identical with 'what it is to be good', the statement 'goodness is good' cannot be predicative, it simply expresses identity. I am not convinced that the key to the interpretation is to be found in Aristotle's relation to Plato. First, it is difficult to say exactly what view Plato took on this matter?[39] Second, in what sense does Aristotle solve problems in Plato's philosophy, i.e. what is really Aristotle's standpoint on this issue? I believe a methodological shortcut can be made if one simply reads the text and takes the platonic examples for what they are, namely examples. This brings us from Plato's philosophy and Aristotle's criticism of it back to Aristotle's own theory.

We learned that Aristotle is not concerned about the identity of the particular thing and its essence. The only passage where the particular thing appears is the statement 'Socrates and what it is to be Socrates are the same',[40] and this passage can, I believe, be understood as an example of what is meant. The ἕκαστον does not mean particular thing. And the examples used in the argument for identity, namely 'goodness itself' and 'being', show that it is not the identity between thing and essence which is discussed, since these examples are not examples of this kind of identity; but how are we then to understand it?

Systematically there is a progression in the arguments for identity. First we learned that if ousia is not identical with its what-being-is, there will be yet another ousia, and this will be prior to the first one. Further, this argument applies to the second ousia as well, i.e. the thesis of non-identity implies an infinite regress. Finally, if knowledge is not of what the thing is, we can have no knowledge at all, and any being will be principally unknowable. These arguments add perfectly together, and when we simplify the argument it says: *if ousia is not identical with its what-being-is, then knowledge of any being is impossible and being principally unknowable*. And this conclusion is evidently unacceptable, therefore ousia must be identical with its what-being-is.

The question 'what is ousia?' has a double meaning. We might ask '*what* is ousia?' and we might ask 'what *is* ousia?' i.e. what is the cause of its existence? If we pose the first question, the answer would be universal-what-being-is, but if we pose the second question the answer would be particular form or what-being-is. What is shown in Z_6 is that there is identity between these two answers.

From an ontological point of view, the thing *is* its ousia, it has being independent of our knowledge of it, it has, so to speak, its own form or what-being-is. But in our attempt to achieve knowledge we ask, 'what is it?' and this question can of course not be answered by the particular what-being-is of a particular thing, since knowledge is of the universal.

Nevertheless, these two answers are not adequately accounted for by the division into existence and essence. The epistemological approach has, if we accept the thesis of non-identity, to do with the 'what' of the thing, and this 'what' has no existence – so why not call it essence? But what is left then – sheer existence? Evidently not, since the problem with the thesis of non-identity is that '*what* the thing is' is not identical with 'what the thing *is*'. The identity posed in Z_6 is not between matter and (universal) form but between the ousia of the particular thing, i.e. its particular form or what-being-is and its universal-what-being-is. The particular what-being-is denotes in a sense both essence and existence, and this ousia would be unknowable if it were not identical with its universal what-being-is. But how are we to understand this identity?

VII

Scaltsas argues[41] that it is identity between the thing and its particular what-being-is which is stated in Z_6. A main argument for this view is that the universal what-being-is is just an abstraction from the particulars, and this abstraction has no being and can never *be* identical with the thing. Another way of putting this is that there is identity between matter and form (given that form and what-being-is are the same). My answer to this argument, in accordance with what is said about identity earlier, is that ταὐτὸν ἐστίν ('is the same' or 'identity') does not necessarily mean 'being the same thing' like the teacher of Alexander and the founder of Lykeion are the same 'thing', namely Aristotle. We might distinguish between being the same in relation to the existence of a thing and in relation to ousia or what-being-is. The teacher of Alexander and the founder of the Peripatetic School are rightly said to be identical, by the fact of the existence of a particular thing. Particular what-being-is and universal what-being-is are not identical in being the same thing, since none of them are just things, they are rather to be understood as causes and principles of things.

Hence, the thesis of identity in Z_6 is to be understood as formal identity rather than numerical. And by formal identity I mean (i) an identity which is guaranteed by a unity – it is not non-numerical in a modern sense of the word (in the sense that it is neither one nor more); (ii) an identity which is guaranteed by an ontological and epistemological principle – not by the existence of a particular thing. Hence, formal identity is in this case understood as *a unitarian ontological and epistemological principle*.

In the end of Z_8 we find the famous and much discussed lines speaking of formal identity:

> "τὸ δ' ἅπαν ἤδη, τὸ τοιόνδε εἶδος ἐν ταῖσδε ταῖς σαρξὶ καὶ ὀστοῖς, Καλλίας καὶ Σωκράτης· καὶ ἕτερον μὲν διὰ τὴν ὕλην (ἑτέρα γάρ), ταὐτὸ δὲ τῷ εἴδει (ἄτομον γὰρ τὸ εἶδος)." 1034a 5-8
>
> "The complete result, such a kind of form in this flesh and bones, is Callias and Socrates. What makes them different is their matter, which is different; but they are the same in form, since their form is indivisible."

The formal identity of Socrates and Callias is not to be understood as a simple identity of their souls, since the soul of Socrates is in fact different from that of Callias. The passage is best explained by the fact that Socrates and Callias are said to be the same as regards their form. This is due to the fact that the particular what-being-is is identical with the universal-what-being-is, and only because this is the case for both Socrates and Callias it is, so to speak, possible to state that they are the same with regard to form.

Contrary to what is stated in the quote, sheer matter cannot be the only 'thing' which differentiates Socrates and Callias, since, as Balme puts it, "Otherness must be formal, even when it is caused by matter and movement"[42]. In an epistemological sense Socrates and Callias are the same, namely 'a man', but this does not mean that they are the same thing. Further, that matter differentiates Socrates and Callias does not necessarily imply that *only* matter differentiates them, they might very well and do in fact possess different particular forms.

VIII

In Z_6 Aristotle takes the thesis of non-identity ad absurdum: If ousia is not identical with its what-being-is, then knowledge of any being is impossible and being principally unknowable. This conclusion is evidently unacceptable, therefore the premise is false. But one might ask, why is this conclusion unacceptable?

If Aristotle were to answer this question, he would presumably refer to the fact that we already have some knowledge, and that it would be absurd to deny this. However, the absurdity attached to the denial of the principle of identity, is, at least to the modern reader, not quite as fatal as the absurdity attached to the denial of the principle of contradiction and the principle of the excluded middle.[43] If these principles are denied, (i) we could not attach one meaning to words and concepts, (ii) we could not draw a clear distinction between 'what is ousia' and 'what is coincidental', and (iii) we could not distinguish between true and false, etc. and eventually, we would even be unable to deny these principles, as the denial presupposes them. Hence, it is impossible to deny them, but the same cannot be said for the thesis of identity in Z_6.

A modern sceptic subjectivist might argue that the denial of the thesis of identity only implies that it is impossible to acquire knowledge of being. However, knowing that it is impossible to obtain knowledge of any being is not itself knowledge of being, but only knowledge of knowledge. The thesis of non-identity is not itself a thesis concerning being, it is a thesis concerning knowledge of being. Hence, it is not self-contradictory to claim non-identity.[44]

Viewed in this light, it is impossible, within Aristotle's metaphysics, to give a satisfactory answer to this question, I believe. Nevertheless, from a historical point of view, it is not only of interest what Aristotle would have replied to Descartes' radical doubt or the thought experiment of brains in vats or the like, since questions like these are not at first hand to be found within the Greek horizon, they are parachronistic. It might be even more interesting to find the seeds which evolve into the flourishing of the philosophy of subject by Descartes, and I believe we find such a seed in Z_6.

In Aristotle we find a dawning consciousness of the possibility of a radical separation of being and knowledge. He is aware of the problem, but at the same time unwilling to take the full consequence of it. The full consequence must have seemed too absurd in order to be taken seriously, since his arguments for the thesis of identity really only appeal to common sense – it is completely implausible that true being (ousia) is principally unknowable and that knowledge has no true object, i.e. is principally impossible. Retrospectively we can find the seed to the much later philosophy of subject. However, to Aristotle himself the possibility of non-identity was just a dead end which had to be closed.

IX

If my interpretation of Z_6 is correct, as I believe it is, we still have some unfinished problems to deal with. First, if each-thing in Z_6 does not mean the particular compound, how does Aristotle mediate between the changeable particular compound and ousia? I am convinced that Aristotle in fact has a solution to this problem and this is to be found in the thesis of identy in H_6. In this sense the theses of identity in Z_6 and H_6 (that matter and form is the same thing) are intimately linked together. Further, the consequence of the thesis in H_6 (that matter is definable) is contradicted by the analysis of the definition of what-being-is (τὸ τί ἦν εἶναι) in the chapters Z_4 and Z_5 which explicitly excludes matter and which leads to Z_6. In the light of these problems it is my task in the following to pursue a unifying interpretation of H_6 which not only places it in relation to Z but displays it as productive to the reading of Z.

Further, the question of identity between form and matter is intimately related to the much discussed question of pure form. If what truly *is* is the particular compound, pure form is an abstraction made by the mind and has no ontological independent status. Hence, the interpretation of H_6 is part of a solution to the question of pure form and has to deal with this issue.

I shall begin by discussing two paradigmatic views on the subject of pure form namely that of Lacey and that of Ryan. Secondly, I shall discuss the new and interesting contribution to the debate of pure form put forward by Balme in his reading of particularly the biological writings and in his interpretation of H_6. Finally, I shall deal with the thesis of identity in H_6.

X

In the beginning of Z, Aristotle introduces the ontological project as the quest for knowledge of the primary being (τὸ πρώτως ὄν) and of what *is* without qualification (ὂν ἁπλῶς). Only ousia satisfies these descriptions, and ousia is thus the object of investigation. In Z_3 we learn that being separate (χωριστόν) and being a-this (τόδε τι) chiefly belong to ousia. Hence, ousia is primary because it is separate and a-this.

Being separate and a-this is often understood as the point where Aristotle falls back into Platonism, since being separate and a-this is taken to denote an independent existence, a thing which exists independently of anything else, and this is named *pure form*. Many interpreters believe that Aristotle actually held this view. Some think it is disastrous to his philosophy, others that it is not, but the overall question is, how far this view is applicable to Aristotle's ontology?

Lacey believes that Aristotle "... was unable to avoid speaking of the form as a kind of entity, even though this was the fault he found in Plato"[45] This is a natural consequence of the fact that "... one of the roles of οὐσία is to be that which is most actual, and since Aristotle equates potentiality with matter οὐσία in this role becomes pure form"[46] And according to Lacey this constitutes a fallacy since "... the notion of form only makes sense in conjunction with that of matter. (...) If we abolish matter we can still go on talking about the shape, but the shape will no longer 'exist', i.e. be an object."[47] Hence, the notion of pure form is applicable to Aristotle but at the same time it is deeply problematic.

This dilemma can be avoided if one pulls one of its horns. Ryan[48] pulls the first one. He notes that χωριστόν has more than one meaning. Ryan lists three senses; (i) "... the characteristic or ability of existing apart from other things, independence of them ..."; (ii) "... the ability not only to exist apart from other things, but to exist apart from matter altogether ..."; and (iii) "... the capability of being thought of or perceived apart from matter ..."[49] Ryan's point is that we only have a fallacy if we, like Lacey, understand χωριστόν in the first or second sense. If, however, we take χωριστόν in the third sense there is no problem, since it is only in thought that form is pure, not ἁπλῶς (without qualification).

However, this solution has the undesirable consequence that form is only separable in thought, in reality it is dependent on matter. This solution subjectifies form, i.e. ousia, and one might ask, what is the ontological status of this pure form, and what is the relation between the particular (form/matter) forms which are dependent on matter and the pure subjective form? We need not go further into these questions, as I believe they are not easily answered within this conception of pure form. If we follow Ryan's route, we escape the Platonic fallacy only to find ourselves in a new one.

I believe a better strategy is to pull the other horn. If we abolish matter, form cannot exist, i.e. be an object. It is necessary once more to take a closer look at the expression χωριστόν. Aristotle distinguishes between τῷ λόγῳ χωριστόν ἐστιν (is separable in formula/definition), and χωριστὸν ἁπλῶς (separate without qualification). Where χωριστὸν ἁπλῶς denotes what is separate without qualification, i.e. ontologically independent, the τῷ λόγῳ χωριστόν ἐστιν denotes what is separable in definition or in formula, i.e. what is separable in thought. This is, I believe, the fundamental difference between these expressions. Hence, the question in relation to the issue of pure form, is what is meant by χωριστὸν ἁπλῶς? Lacey and Ryan understand χωριστὸν ἁπλῶς in the sense *independent existence*. However, I believe another interpretation is possible.

The ἁπλῶς which we translate 'without qualification' is, I believe, by Lacey and Ryan understood as an absolute, rather than a relative expression. Ἁπλῶς is often taken in contrast to expressions like πρός τι (in relation to something) or πρὸς ἡμᾶς (regarding us), i.e. in the sense 'not in relation to anything but absolutely'. However, if it is understood as an absolute in the expression χωριστὸν ἁπλῶς, its opposite is τῷ λόγῳ χωριστόν ἐστιν. But the τῷ λόγῳ χωριστόν ἐστιν is not a relative like πρός τι or πρὸς ἡμᾶς. The τῷ λόγῳ does not place the χωριστόν in relation to anything, it delimits it and cannot, as I see it, function as a relative sense in contrast to an absolute one.

Instead I shall suggest another less specific interpretation of ἁπλῶς, as ἁπλῶς without reference to an opposite relative is possible. We might then translate it 'simply' or 'plainly' and the χωριστὸν ἁπλῶς would then be translated 'simply separate' or 'plainly separate'. However, these translations have certain implications in English and the question is, can we maintain the use of 'separate without qualification'?

'Without qualification' can mean 'absolute' in the sense 'not in relation to anything', but it also has a weaker sense, as it it i.e. can mean 'without further specification'. In relation to the whole expression it makes a significant difference. Χωριστὸν ἁπλῶς in one sense means 'separate' in an absolute sense, denoting that which *is,* that which exists without reference to anything else, i.e. independently, in contrast to any relative being. Χωριστὸν ἁπλῶς in the weaker sense means 'separate without further specifications', it does not denote an absolute independence regarding its existence but just plainly and simply separateness. Further, it has to be read in relation to its context, i.e. being *separate as regards what it is,* namely an ontological principle. It *is* independent as ontological principle, not as an existing thing

Hence this interpretation follows Ryan, in that existence is not to be ascribed to pure form, like Lacey claims. However, pure form has more than a pure subjective status. It is, I believe, to be understood as an ontological principle, i.e. it has some sort of non-subjective status[50], and this is achieved through this minimalist reading of χωριστὸν ἁπλῶς.[51]

XI

The study of Aristotle's biological works leads Balme to question the old assumption that Aristotle's biology is essentialistic. The denial of essentialism is the denial of the view which holds that "… each animal's growth is directed primarily towards the form of the species; that its essence prescribes its form; and that animal form excludes material accidents such as eye colour."[52]

A thorough reading of De Generatione Animalium has shown that animals do not develop in order to realise a species-essence, they develop towards parental likeness,[53] which includes non-essential likeness such as sex and eye colour. The common form, i.e. the species, is due to a generalisation of the common features which accompany a given group of animals. Hence, the teleology is explicable as what benefits an animal of this kind. "The fact that individuals develop in their most advantageous way in given circumstances, within the limits of the form inherited from their parents, is enough to explain the existence of species in Aristotle's sense of it."[54] The individual does not develop in accordance with species, species is possible due to the fact that there actually is something common in the development in a certain group, "… species membership is a consequential, not a primary cause in animal reproduction and growth."[55]

All differences and likenesses are formal in the sense that matter, being indeterminable, cannot be ascribed to these.[56] Hence, all differences are in a sense formal. However, what-being-is (i.e. essence in Balme's vocabulary) is, according to Z_{4-5}, what first and foremost is definable, and the definition of what-being-is rules out matter. Consequently, form and what-being-is is not the same, in fact "... the essence need not be a morphological concept at all. At the most abstract level the essence of a man is just rational soul, of a house it is just shelter."[57]

Hence, according to Balme there is only a what-being-is of such a thing which is not a snub (i.e. a compound). On the other hand, the form which is studied in Z and used in GA is the form of a compound, which is not understood totally independent of matter, as Balme's study of e.g. GA shows. It is the inherited form which is to be taken into account for the genesis and growth of animals, and not what-being-is. Hence, if the conclusion of Z_{4-5} (that only what-being-is is definable and that the definition excludes matter) then, either the concept of form as inherited form is wrong (i.e. a theory of pure form must be applicable to Aristotle's metaphysics), or philosophy is principally unable to account for the physical, changeable world.

However, if we jump to H_3 we learn that,

"ὥστ' οὐσίας ἔστι μὲν ἧς ἐνδέχεται εἶναι ὅρον καὶ λόγον, οἷον τῆς συνθέτου, ἐάν τε αἰσθητὴ ἐάν τε νοητὴ ᾖ·" 1043b 28-30

"Hence, one kind of ousia, namely the composite, may have a definition and a formula – this might be sensible or intelligible."

And in H_6 we learn more about how matter is thought to be applied to the definition.

"ἔστι δ', ὥσπερ εἴρηται, ἡ ἐσχάτη ὕλη καὶ ἡ μορφὴ ταὐτὸ καὶ ἕν, δυνάμει, τὸ δὲ ἐνεργείᾳ, ..." 1045b 17-19

"But, as has been said, the final matter and the shape are one and the same, one potentially and the other actually"

The compound is definable since the matter when formed *is* its form, matter is potentiality but when it is actualised into something it *is* in a sense actual, i.e. identical with its actuality, i.e. its form. But how is this account of definition to be seen in relation to the one given for definition of what-being-is in Z_{4-5}?

Bostock believes that the two different accounts of definition are due to a development in Aristotle's thought, maintaining that the one given in H is the latest. Balme, on the other hand, interprets the account of definition in Z as aporetic. On the one hand, Z states that there is no definition of specific compounds, i.e. individual, natural things. On the other hand, there is no question about the fact that Aristotle really believes philosophy to be a science of what *is*. Hence, what Z really does is to pose an aporia which eventually is to be solved in H_6. However, I believe Balme is right in his insisting on the unity of these two accounts of definition, though I do believe that his unity is not unitarian enough. According to Balme, Z and H are to be read together, but he sees Z as holding an impossible view which has to be altered, and this is done in H. Opposed to this, I shall try to read the accounts of definition in Z and H as not contradictory but complementary.

XII

Balme, and before him Rorty, believes that H_6 is to be taken into account for the idea that matter is definable, i.e. when matter is the matter of the compound. Let us take a closer look at the text.

It is not just matter which is identical with the shape of the thing, it is ἡ ἐσχάτη ὕλη (the final matter). As the word indicates, ὕλη[58] is not anything or some thing in particular, it *is* potentially this or that. Like other concepts, ὕλη functions on several levels from ἡ ἐσχάτη ὕλη to ἡ πρώτη ὕλη[59] (the primary matter). The primary matter is formed into earth, air, fire, or water, these again may be formed into a tree which is cut down and made into timber which again is shaped by the cabinetmaker into a chair, etc.[60] Both the primary matter, the elements, and the tree are all matter but on different levels. The primary matter *is* nothing, it is sheer potentiality (it has to be formed through a chain of forming in order to finally be something). Contrary to this the final matter is the matter shaped into actually being something. This matter has actualised its potential and is now identical with what it is, i.e. its form.

This account of matter is of interest in relation to Balme's understanding of H_6. According to him what is defined in H_6 is not a compound in change (i.e. a thing in time) it is a compound taken as if frozen at a given moment.[61] When frozen at a given moment the thing has no past and no future; it has no coming to be and no passing away; it is pure actuality and pure lack of potentiality. Put in this strange milieu Socrates is not two things, matter and form, body and soul, he is one single, unitary actuality. Hence, according to Balme, it is not matter as such, or even the matter of the compound as such which is definable, the only definable matter is that which in a moment is actualised and shaped.

If we take away change, coming to be, and passing away, it is obvious that there is no need for the concepts designed to deal with change, namely matter and form, and it should come as no surprise that the one under these circumstances can be reduced to the other. However, I do believe we have to question if this really can be Aristotle's view. Is it possible that Aristotle is content with a definition which is able to grasp the individual, particular thing as frozen at a given moment? Will it not follow that the definition of e.g. Socrates might change through his lifetime? and if so, that no definition of the living Socrates is possible? I believe this view is obviously unacceptable and I shall offer another interpretation of the passage in H_6.

If we go back to H_3 and read the quote in connection with the lines which follow:

> "ὥστ' οὐσίας ἔστι μὲν ἧς ἐνδέχεται εἶναι ὅρον καὶ λόγον, οἷον τῆς συνθέτου, ἐάν τε αἰσθητὴ ἐάν τε νοητὴ ᾖ· ἐξ ὧν δ' αὕτη πρώτων, οὐκέτι, εἴπερ τὶ κατὰ τινὸς σημαίνει ὁ λόγος ὁ ὁριστικὸς καὶ δεῖ τὸ μὲν ὥσπερ ὕλην εἶναι τὸ δὲ ὡς μορφήν" 1043b 28-32
>
> "Hence, one kind of ousia, namely the composite, may have a definition and a formula – this might be sensible or intelligible. But what it is primarily composed of may not, since the defining formula predicates one thing of another; one must play the part of matter and one the part of form."

Here we learn that the definition of the compound, which Aristotle apparently believes is possible, has the form τὶ κατὰ τινὸς σημαίνει (one thing predicated of another). However, in relation to predicating the form of matter, the formula 'one thing predicated of another' does not quite function as an adequate expression, since neither the form nor the matter taken separately *are* anything i.e. exist as separate things. We speak of them as though they were, but they are not. And in H_6 we learn that ontologically speaking they are identical, i.e. two aspects which we divide in order to obtain knowledge of changeable things, but nevertheless they remain two aspects of one unitarian being.

Further, the quotation shows that Balme is right in his observation that it is not the primary components, e.g. matter as such, which are included in the definition but only the in-formed matter. But are we on the basis of this observation ready to conclude that it is the particular thing frozen at a given moment which is definable, according to Aristotle? I believe we must change our perspective on the issue.

When Aristotle declares that 'the final matter and the shape are one and the same thing', it is of utmost importance to acknowledge that it is the 'final matter' which is spoken of, i.e. it is the in-formed matter which is identical with its form. It is not Socrates' potential ability to grow grey hair or develop senility, etc. It is the actualised potentiality which is identical with its form and therefore definable. But what is actualised potentiality? is it potentiality or actuality or both? It is evidently not both and it is not potentiality, it must be sheer actuality in order to be definable. Hence, matter which is potentiality is definable only when it is ontologically transformed into form, i.e. actualised. This leads Balme to assume that what is definable is the concrete, final, i.e. actualised matter.

What is meant, I believe, is that the particular thing is definable with regard to *what* it is, i.e. its what-being-is, since the particular thing is only one thing with regard to *what it is*. Hence, the decisive factor in my interpretation of H_6 in relation to that of Balme is, what is the relation between form and what-being-is?

XIII

Balme operates with a weak conception of what-being-is. According to him, animals do not develop in accordance with an essential inner nature or in order to develop an entelechy and consequently the conception of essence as "that which has belonged to X so that it is X"[62] does not apply to Aristotle's understanding of τὸ τί ἐν εἶναι (what-being-is). Balme understands what-being-is purely as a teleological concept naming the telos of changeable things, e.g. the what-being-is of house is shelter and of man it is rational soul, etc. and he quite neglects the ontological understanding of what-being-is, he sees what-being-is as a product of man which has no direct ontological equivalent in the nature of things.

In the first part of this article I have argued that what-being-is is a highly variable neologism designed to cover more than just one single sense. There is an ontological as well as an epistemological interpretation which by no means exclude one another. In the ontological sense what-being-is denotes *the being of what is the underlying, unchangeable, and persistent being in question.* This is understood not as an existentiological but as an ontological ἀρχή. And in the epistemological sense the what-being-is denotes a conceptual *what* which functions as a preconceived knowledge in order to experience.

In Z_{4-5}, we learn that the definition of what-being-is excludes matter, that the compound as compound has no definition in the true sense of the word. This is of course aporetic, but the aporia is not, I believe, solved the way Balme thinks. The solution is not that the compound is definable if we take it as if frozen, it is that the actualised thing is a unity with regard to *what it is,* as long as it is; Socrates is *what* he is for as long as he is, i.e. from his birth to his death. The matter of Socrates is actualised into what he is during his whole lifetime. Aristotle was acquainted with the fact that the matter of the body changes; we eat, cut our hair and nails, etc. Nevertheless the matter Socrates consists of is actually him (as well as he is a man).

I do not believe that Aristotle by ἡ ἐσχάτη ὕλη (final matter) just refers to concrete flesh and bones, but that the ἐσχάτη denotes *the matter which is matter of each actual thing in question.* The ἡ ἐσχάτη ὕλη is the matter of e.g. Socrates in so far as he is *what* he is, i.e. a man. Socrates is what he is as he is the actualised potential being, and as actualised he is one thing, namely *what he is.* Ἡ ἐσχάτη ὕλη is not just the concrete sum of the matter of a thing taken at a frozen moment, it is the matter which in the compound is actualised into something, i.e. into some kind of thing.

This understanding of ἡ ἐσχάτη ὕλη would be further supported if we were to attempt to give a definition of Socrates. His definition would be indifferent to whether his hair is dark or grey, whether he is thick or thin, tall or small etc. In fact it is indifferent to his matter in all other respects than the fact that he is actually a man. Further, Aristotle did not believe that it is possible to give a definition of the particular, in fact, the definition of man is in this respect the definition of Socrates, i.e. the actual Socrates is covered by the definition.

The discrepancy in the accounts of definition in Z_{4-5} and in H_6 is not really a discrepancy in the understanding of definition as much as it is a discrepancy in the understanding of matter. In Z_{4-5} Aristotle conducts a logical analysis of what-being-is. He is not first of all interested in excluding matter from the definition but in a conceptual analysis of what-being-is and its definition, and as an added bonus, we might say, matter is excluded from the definition. It is, however, not ἡ ἐσχάτη ὕλη which is excluded but matter in the sense of potentiality. Hence, we might very well read H_6 in extension of Z_{4-5} and there is no discrepancy in the two accounts of definition.

XIV

This brings us to the question, what is meant by identity? In interpreting the thesis of identity in Z_6 I discussed whether identity is to be understood as either formal or numerical and further what is meant by these conceptions of identity. I found that formal identity is not to be understood as non-numerical in a modern sense of the word, it denotes something being one and the same in form, i.e. being in principle one, whereas numerical identity denotes the identity of a countable thing, i.e. one thing among others.

If we take a closer look at the above quoted passage where the thesis of identity is put forward we find that 'final matter' and 'shape' is *one and the same* (ταὐτὸ καὶ ἕν). On the face of it we might apply both the formal and the numerical sense of identity to this formulation, they are, however, not equally productive. From an ontological point of view it is not very illuminating to learn that the particular thing is both its matter and its shape, and in this sense that the particular thing is a unity and that the final matter and the form *is* the same countable thing – we already know this, as this is how Aristotle understands and conceptualises a thing. What is of interest is *what makes it one* or *why it is one* and this is the form which in a formal sense is identical with the final matter. Hence, the identity claimed in H_6 Is most likely the very same as the one claimed in Z_6, namely formal identity.

XV

The thesis of identity in Z_6 claims that the universal form is identical with the particular form, i.e. that the universal definition does in fact define something, namely the ousia of the particular things. Further, the ontological principle of the particular thing is its particular form which again according to the thesis of identity in H_6 is identical with the final matter. In this sense the two theses of identity in Z_6 and H_6 bridge the gap between the universal form or what-being-is and the existing particular thing.

However, this leaves us with the problem of understanding the overall philosophical outlook behinde the theses of identity and it challanges us to give a more precise and profound account of how Aristotle believed the so called 8th aporia, that only individuals exist and knowledge is of what is universal, to be solved. This question I will deal with in my forthcoming article *"Primary Philosophy as Gradual Ontology"*.

Notes:
1. Tredennick 1933 bd. I p. 331.
2. Boniz 1991 Bd. II p. 21.
3. Tricot 1070, p. 370. Tricot's translation is, however, not suitable, since it cannot be 'any being' which is identical with its what-being-is, since what is thought of as each-thing is what "is thought to be nothing else but its own ousia" and this rules out what is not an ousia, e.g. the 'is' of the secondary categories.
4. Frede/Patzig 1988, Bd. II, pp. 87-88.
5. Bassenge 1960.
6. For a full account of these interpretations and especially the arguments against the substantivized τί, see Bassenge 1960, pp. 19-25.
7. Arpe 1938.
8. Naturally, Socrates did not invent the question τί ἐστι? It was a common way of asking for knowledge of any kind of thing, it was as common and widely used as the English 'what is it?' However, the Socratic question does not ask for just any kind of knowledge, it asks 'what is justice?', 'what is beauty?', etc. i.e. he asks for the definition.
9. Weidemann, 1982, pp. 180-181.
10. Ross follows Schwengler in distinguishing three accounts of the imperfect, namely (i) as a philosophical imperfect, (ii) as imperfect of duration and (iii) as "an expression of Aristotle's doctrine of the existence of form before its embodiment in a particular matter." (Ross 1924, bd. I p. 127) Arpe proposes yet another sense, namely as "Imperfekt der gedanklichen Voraussetzung" (Arpe 1938, p. 17).
11. However, the definition of the philosophical imperfect given by Ross, is not very philosophical. This label seems only to be chosen as a result of the fact that this imperfect appears in a philosophical text.
12. Ross 1924, bd. I p. 127.
13. E.g. ἐπεὶ δ' ἦσαν τρεῖς οὐσίαι (1071b 3) (directly translated, "since there were three kinds of ousiai" but the meaning is, "since there are, as we saw, three kinds of ousiai") For further examples see, Bassenge 1960 p. 26.
14. Schwyzler,1950, bd.II 2, p. 279.
15. Bassenge 1960, p. 213
16. A similar use of aspect is found in French in the distinction between l'imparfait and le passé simple.
17. Ross 1924, bd. II p. 188. An example of this is found in Z_{15} "Ἐπεὶ δ' ἡ οὐσία ἑτέρα, τό τε σύνολον καὶ ὁ λόγος (λέγυ δ' ὅτι ἡ μὲν οὕτως ἐστὶν οὐσία, σὺν τῇ ὕλῃ συνειλημμένος ὁ λόγος, ἡ δ' ὁ λόγος ὅλως), ὅσαι μὲν οὖν οὕτω λέγονται, τούτων μέν ἔστι φθορά (καὶ γὰρ γένεσις), τοῦ δὲ λόγου οὐκ ἔστιν οὕτως ὥστε φθείρεσθαι (οὐδὲ γὰρ γένεσις, οὐ γὰρ γίγνεται τὸ οἰκίᾳ εἶναι ἀλλὰ τὸ τῇδε τῇ οἰκίᾳ), ἀλλ' ἄνευ γενέσεως καὶ φθορᾶς εἰσὶ καὶ οὐκ εἰσίν· δέδεικται γὰρ ὅτι οὐδεὶς ταῦτα γεννᾷ οὐδὲ ποιεῖ" 1039b 20-27 ("The combined whole and the formula are different ousiai, (I mean, one being an ousia in that it is the formula taken together with the matter, while the other is the formula on its own). Accordingly the combined whole may cease to be (since it may also come to be), but there is no ceasing to be of the formula, in the sense that it is ever in the process of ceasing to be. (For it cannot come to be either. Being for a house cannot come to be; only being for this particular house). Rather, such ousiai are or are not without coming to be or ceasing to be, for we have shown that one cannot create or produce them.").
18. Ein jeweiliges Sein.
19. As mentioned earlier the ontological ἀρχή is not itself a thing, but is to be thought of as an ontological precondition for the thing.

20. Kahn C.H. 1976 and 1966.
21. Plato's use of ontological and epistemological concepts and his insisting on their interrelation is adopted by Aristotle. Several passages show this, e.g. 1029a 33-b13. What is new in Aristotle is not the rejection of this, but his dismissal of Plato's hypostatizing of ideas.
22. Se also Bassenge 1960, p. 209.
23. As the English language has no natural way of distinguishing between the senses of ὄν and τὸ ὄντο I shall follow the tradition which writes 'Being' with a capital B.
24. 1029b 13.
25. It has been assumed by e.g. Bostock (1994, p. 86) that we have to choose between three senses of λογικῶς, (i) λόγος could mean definition, and Z_{4-5} would then deal with a definition of what-being-is; and (ii) λογικῶς could refer to analysis concerning the language, and eventually (iii) the distinction of λογικῶς μὲν ... and φυσικῶς δὲ ... in the *Physics* (204b 4 and 204b 10) could be applied to Z. This would mean that the analysis of Z_{4-5} is concerned with the concept of what-being-is. However, I do not believe that these senses contradict each other, on the contrary, they supplement each other.
26. The relation of the two latter senses of what-being-is is obviously closely related to the question of definition. I am trying to clear up this issue in a forthcoming article: *The Non-Classificatory Definition in Aristotle*.
27. There is some disagreement as to the authenticity of this book. Nevertheless, I treat it as authentic in its core, i.e. even though it is a work of a disciple and not of Aristotle's hand it is Aristotelian in its core and does in fact express Aristotle's understanding of e.g. identity.
28. 1018a 6-7
29. 1034a 5-8.
30. 1031a 16-18.
31. 1031a 19-24, 1031a 24-28.
32. A more elaborate account is given by e.g. Frede/Patzig, 1988, Bd. II, and Bostock 1994.
33. This sense of identity is accounted for at 1017b 27-ff.
34. In outline, I follow Bostock (1994) in his interpretation of the given examples, they are neither meant as a giving in to Plato's philosophy, nor as a critique of it or the like, but plainly and simply as one out of many possible examples of a theory of ousia.
35. 1031b 28-30.
36. this argument is generally referred to as the third man argument.
37. This is a thesis which is not established in Z_6, it is rather assumed as a natural premise for the whole argument.
38. This theme has been vividly debated since Owen (1965) interpreted Z_6 in this way. He takes Aristotle to deny two of Plato's theses, namely the thesis of non-identity and the thesis of self-predication. Owen understands Aristotle's thesis of identity as identity between the particular thing and its essence. However, such an identity leaves us with another problem, namely the problem that the proposition 'Socrates is a man' consequently cannot be predicative, it must, if identity is taken in this sense, be identifying. For a newer account and discussion of this theme see Scaltsas 1994, pp. 121-165.
39. see e.g. Allen, 1978.
40. 1032a 8.
41. Scaltsas, 1994, chapter 6.
42. Balme, 1987, p. 305.
43. Most of Γ is devoted to the indirect proof of these principles. The analysis includes in a way the logical principle of identity (A is A) which is presupposed but never explicitly dealt with by Aristotle.

44. There are of course philosophers who believe that sceptic subjectivism and solipsism are self-contradictory. However, we shall not deal with this, but simply assume that sceptic subjectivism is not wrong because of a logical inconsistency.
45. Lacey 1965 p. 66.
46. ibid. 66.
47. ibid. 67.
48. Ryan, 1973.
49. ibid. pp. 213-214.
50. I refer to the distinction 'subjective/objective' only because of its widespread use, and because the reader presumably might ask if I prescribe a subjective or an objective sense to pure form. However, what is 'subjective' has no real existence, it is only found within the thought of the subject. And what is objective is detectable through empiria, i.e. exists. The distinction leaves no room for what is neither subjective nor existent, but this is exactly what I believe pure form to be. The distinction has its own history (although it is very interesting, there is no room for it here) and its own metaphysical preconceptions which function well within the tradition of the philosophy of subject, but leave the historian of philosophy with an anachronistic figure of thought. Hence it is not without reluctance that I refer to the distinction.

    I shall use 'subjective' in the common sense, but if I were to use 'objective' it would have to be in a reduced sense, meaning just 'non-subjective', i.e. without prescribing existence to what is objective. This is, however, not in accordance with the common use, and might most likely cause miscomprehensions, I shall therefore just use 'subjective' and 'non-subjective'.
51. Another way of avoiding Ryan's interpretation is to take τῷ λόγῳ χωριστόν in another sense. Τῷ λόγῳ χωριστόν is translated into 'separable in formula/definition', and Ryan understands this as 'separable in thought', i.e. in a subjective sense. However, λόγος means 'word', 'formula', 'definition', 'order', 'reason', etc. etc. (For a fuller account of λόγος see e.g. Guthrie I 1962 pp. 419 ff.). It is difficult to enumerate all its senses and clearly impossible to find one word in the modern languages which covers its sense. Nevertheless, the listed translations show that λόγος not only is applicable to subjective conceptual senses but likewise to what we might call non-subjective ontological senses. And, I believe, albeit Aristotle's use of λόγος in the sense of 'definition' and 'formula', that it is wrong to renounce all non-subjective meaning to Aristotle's use of λογος . Hence, instead of translating ἐν τῷ λογῷ into 'in thought' (i.e. in a subjective sense), we might more accurately translate it into 'in reason' ('ratio' is a translation of 'λόγος ') (It must here be remembered that 'reason' has a subjective as well as a non-subjective sense). This reading of τῷ λόγῳ χωριστόν would, as my reading of χωριστὸν ἁπλῶς, do the job, namely on the one hand to renounce existence to pure form and on the other give form some ontological status. However, it would not be pure form, since what is separable is not separate. Like the convex and the concave side of a concave mirror is separable in thought but not in reality, so is the form separable but not separate according to this interpretation. Nevertheless, I find χωριστὸν ἁπλῶς the more likely of the two, as I am not totally convinced that τῷ λόγω has a non-subjective sense here and further, I strongly believe that there is room for a conception of pure form in Aristotle's metaphysics.
52. Balme 1987 p. 291.
53. "The male semen contributes nothing somatic to the fetus, but only 'form' through the medium of 'movements' which it sets up in the uterine blood. Since the semen is drawn from the male's blood at the moment when it is about to be diversified into tissues and limbs (GA1I. 726b10, II. 737a18), its movements control the embryo's development in conformity with the parent's individual attributes." (Blame 1987, p. 312).
54. ibid. p. 291.

55. ibid. p. 293.
56. Z_3.
57. Balme 1987 p. 294.
58. Apart from tree and wood, ὕλη means timber, firewood, and even material and matter. It is obvious in relation to these senses that Aristotle uses the word in the sense of what something can be made of.
59. e.g. 1044a 15-, 1049a 25-.
60. Like Aristotle I find it much easier to illustrate the point using artefacts.
61. Balme 1987 p. 310.
62. Balme 1987 p. 306.

Selected Literature:

Allen, R.E. *"Participation and Predication in Plato's Middle Dialogues"*, in G. Vlastos: *"Plato. A Collection of Critical Essays"* Vol. I. Univ. of Notre Dame Press, 1978.
Aristotle. *"Metaphysics"* by W.D. Ross, Oxford 1924.
Aristotle. *"Metaphysics"* translated by H.Tredennick, Loeb Classical Library, London 1933.
Aristote. *"La Métaphysique"*, Paris 1970.
Aristoteles. *"Metaphysik Z"* by M. Frede & G. Patzig, C.H. Beck, München 1988.
Aristoteles. *"Metaphysik"* by W. Christ & H. Seidl, Felix Meiner, Hamburg 1991.
Arpe, C. *"Das τί ἦν εἶναι bei Aristoteles"*, Hamburg 1938.
Bassenge, F. *"Das τὸ ἑνὶ εἶναι, τὸ ἀγαθῷ εἶναι etc. etc. und das τὸ τί ἦν εἶναι bei Aristoteles"* Philologus CIV 1960.
Balme, D.M. *"Aristotle's Biology was not Essentialist"* in Gotthelf, A. & Lennox, J.G. (ed.) *'Philosophical Issues in Aristotle's Biology'*, Cambridge 1987.
Balme, D.M. *"Aristotle's use of division and differentiae"* in Gotthelf, A. & Lennox, J.G. (ed.) *'Philosophical Issues in Aristotle's Biology'*, Cambridge 1987.
Balme, D.M. *"The Place of biology in Aristotle's philosophy"* in Gotthelf, A. & Lennox, J.G. (ed.) *'Philosophical Issues in Aristotle's Biology'*, Cambridge 1987.
Kahn, C.H. *"The Greek verb 'to be' and the concept of Being"*, Foundation of Language 2, 1966.
Kahn, C.H. *"Why Existence does not Emerge as a Distinct Concept in Greek Philosophy"*, Archiv für Geschichte der Philosophie 58, 1976.
Lacey, A.R. *"Οὐσία and Form in Aristotle"*, Pronesis 10 1965.
Lowe, E.J. *"A Survey of Metaphysics"* Oxford, 2002.
Moreland, J.P. *"Universals"* Acumen, 2001.
Owen, G.E.L. *"Aristotle on the Snares of Ontology"*, in *"New Essays on Plato and Aristotle"*, ed. by Bambrough, Renford, Routledge & Kegan Paul Ltd., London 1965.
Rorty, R. *"Genus as Matter: A Reading of Metaphysics Z-H"* Exegesis and Argument, Assen, Netherlands 1973.
Ryan, E.E. *"Pure Form in Aristotle"* Phronesis 18, 1973.
Scaltsas, T. *"Substances and Universals in Aristotle's Metaphysics"*, London 1994.
Scaltsas, T. *"Substantial Holism"* (Scaltsas, T. Charles, D. og Gill, M.L. *Unity, Identity, and Explanation In Aristotle's Metaphysics*, Oxford Clarendon Press 2001)
Schwyzler. *"Griechische Grammatik"* München, 1950.
Weidemann, H. *"Τόδε τι und τί ἦν εἶναι, Überlegung zu Aristoteles Metaphysik Z4"* Hermes 110, 1982.

DER BEGRIFF DER SITTLICHEN VERNUNFT BEI DEM JUNGEN HEGEL

Peter Wolsing

Süddänische Universität

I. Der Streit um den Standpunkt des jungen Hegel

Ein Blick auf die Erscheinungen zur Hegelforschung in den letzten Jahren bezeugt, daß das Aufsuchen der Inspirationsquellen des jungen Hegel noch nicht zu Ende gekommen ist. Ein Grund, weshalb diese Frage noch nicht hinreichend beantwortet ist, scheint damit zusammenzuhängen, daß das Denken des jungen Hegel in Frankfurt – und besonders in Bern – noch nicht die spekulative Reife erreicht hatte. Wie bekannt, kam erst in Jena unter Schellings Einfluß ein explizit philosophisches Programm auf die Tagesordnung[1]. Von da an entwickelte Hegel seine eigene philosophische Position in der Auseinandersetzung mit Philosophen, die ausdrücklich mit Namen genannt wurden.

Seit Dieter Henrichs Untersuchung in den Sechzigerjahren ist es eine gängige Auffassung, daß Hegel im letzten Jahr in Tübingen und in Bern als dezidierter Kantianer auftrat und sich erst unter Hölderlins Einfluß beim Umzug nach Frankfurt 1797 dessen Vereinigungsphilosophie zuwandte[2]. In Frankfurt reifte allmählich der neue Standpunkt, aus dem die Kritik an Kants und Fichtes Reflexionsphilosophien hervorwuchs. Neuere Erscheinungen modifizierten zwar, aber bleiben im Großen und Ganzen der These von einem Bruch in Hegels frühem Denken treu[3]. So hält Bondeli Hegels Kantkritik in den Jenaer Jahren für das Ergebnis einer längeren Aneignung und Ablehnung von Kants praktischer Philosophie und meint, einen dauernden Einfluß von dem Vorgänger in Hegels späterem Denken zu erblicken. Bondeli spricht von einem "Hegelschen Kantianismus" in Hegels späterem System. Trotz der Unterstellung von Kantianismus auch in Hegels Berner Schriften gesteht Bondeli zu, daß die Klarheit über Motive und alle argumentatorischen Schritte in Hegels Entwicklung noch fehlt. Viele Gestalten kommen hier in Betracht, besonders Rousseau, Spinoza, Schelling und Fichte.

Indessen scheinen Bondelis Untersuchungen an einem zu starken Festhalten an den philosophischen Quellen zu Hegels Denken zu leiden. Wird dagegen ernstgenommen, daß Hegel in Tübingen und Bern noch wenig philosophisch reflektierte, mindestens interessierter an Kultur- und Gesellschaftskritik als an philosophischer Spekulation war, zeigt sich ein modifizierteres Bild von der Gedankenwelt des Jünglings. Ein Blick auf die vielen zerstreuten historischen und sozialen Studien bezeugt, daß Hegel um Lebens- und Gemeinschaftsideale kreiste, deren Vorbilder er in der Vergangenheit – im Urchristentum und der antiken Polis – suchte. Zwar ist diese Entdeckung nicht neu; von Dilthey[4] und Lukács bis Habermas ist ständig Hegels Interesse an politischen und sozialen Fragen unterstrichen worden. Was aber noch fehlt, ist der entscheidende Hinweis, daß diese Gemeinschaftsideale streng genommen mit der Unterstellung von Kantianismus bei dem Berner Hegel unverträglich sind. Mit Hegels Suche nach der Idee von einer Gemeinschaft, die seine Tübinger und Berner Studien überall leitete, wird in der folgenden Untersuchung die These vertreten, daß der junge Hegel immer aus der Vorstellung von einer 'Lebensganzheit' gedacht hatte, daß also eigentlich nicht von einem Bruch in seiner philosophischen Entwicklung in den Neunzigerjahren gesprochen werden kann, wie es Henrich und Andere getan haben. Es wird zu zeigen versucht, daß Hegels Kantianismus deshalb von besonderer Art ist.

II. Kontinuität in Hegels Jugendschriften

Meine Argumente gegen eine zu starke kantianische Interpretation von Hegels Jugendschriften soll für die Auffassung sprechen, daß es keine nennenswerten Brüche in Hegels 'Weg zum System' bis 1800 gibt. Gegen Dieter Henrichs Unterstellung von Kantianismus in Hegels Berner Schriften[5] und folglich von einem Bruch beim Umzug nach Frankfurt hoffe ich, belegen zu können, daß sich Hegel schon in seinen Berner Studien zum antiken Volksleben, zur Politik und zur mythologischen Volksreligion an einem pantheistischen Gedanken von einem Ganzen orientierte, der die Grundlage für ein sittliches Lebensideal bildet, demzufolge sich Freiheit im Gemeinschaftsleben statt in der individuellen Selbstbestimmung der Autonomieethik verwirklicht. Wohl ist Kants praktische Philosophie der philosophische Ausgangspunkt für Hegel in Bern und Tübingen, aber die antiken Lebensformen dienten für ihn nicht, wie Henrich meint, als Beispiele eines 'Freiheitsgeistes', die in der Moderne individuelle Autonomie bedeuten müssen.[6] In dem kantischen Freiheitsgeist entdeckte Hegel das Aufklärungspotential dazu, daß das Individuum *von* damaliger positivreligiöser und politischer Unterdrückung *zu* einem Leben in einer wahren Gemeinschaft befreit werden kann.

Gewiß prägte das Wiedersehen mit Hölderlin in Frankfurt merkbar Hegels Entwicklung, aber meines Erachtens bestand der entscheidende Einfluß des Freundes darin, Hegel von seinen antiken Vorbildern loszumachen und ihn mit der Gegenwart zu konfrontieren. Erst mit Hölderlin begannen Spinoza, Fichte und Kants ästhetische Schriften eine eigentliche Rolle zu spielen. Die Vision von der Vereinigung, in der Hegel das sittliche Ideal in der entzweiten Gegenwart erfüllt sah, war schon in der Tübinger und Berner Zeit im Spiel. Kontinuität und Einheit in Hegels Jugendschriften geben sich dann zu erkennen, wenn pointiert wird, daß in den Berner Schriften schon latent die Kritik an der modernen entzweiten und atomisierten Gesellschaft liegt, die Hegel erst in den Frankfurter Manuskripten in seiner Auseinandersetzung mit Kants individualistischer Ethik philosophisch formulierte.

III. Subjektivität oder Sein. Der Freiheitsgeist des Deutschen Idealismus

Dieter Henrich weist die innere Beziehung zwischen dem Deutschen Idealismus und der Französischen Revolution auf. Die gesellschaftliche Revolution müsse auf einer philosophischen Theorie basieren, um den Status als weltgeschichtliche Begebenheit zu bekommen[7]. Nicht so sehr den materiellen Voraussetzungen der kapitalistischen Produktionsweise, sondern der Innerlichkeit und Spontaneität, die das deutsche Bildungssystem in der protestantischen Kultur wachgerufen hatte, wurde mit Rousseau als aktuellem Anstoß – u.a. von Kant, Jacobi und Fichte philosophisher Ausdruck gegeben in der gemeinsamen Überzeugung, daß ein zeitgemäßes philosophisches System notwendig das Ich-Subjekt als Achse haben müsse.

Henrich unterstellt so dem ganzen Deutschen Idealismus eine für alles Philosophieren grundlegende Absicht, nämlich "die inneren Bewegungen im Leben zu greifen, die auf Vernunft als einer einfachen, einheitlichen Struktur gründen"[8]. Aber darin favorisiert er offenbar Kants und Fichtes Betonung des Ichs als der Quelle der selbstbewußten, freien Handlung. Folglich scheint Fichtes 'Tathandlung' eine Abglanz der politisch-revolutionären Machtergreifung zu sein, wie sie innerhalb eines theoretischen Begründungszusammenhanges aussehen muß. Hat die praktische Vernunft indessen Primat über die subjektive Reflexion, dann muß auch nach dem objektiven Lebenszusammenhang, in die die Handlung eingreift, gefragt werden. Rührt die *Kraft* der Veränderung von der Erfahrung des freien Selbstsetzens im Ich her, so erscheint auch eine normative Idee für eine konkrete Umgestaltung der gesellschaftlichen Wirklichkeit, nämlich in der besonderen Einsicht, die dem Selbstbewußtsein eigentümlich ist: Die Selbsttransparenz, mit der das Ich in seinen intellektuellen Leistungen unmittelbar für sich auftritt, soll auch für das institutionelle System eines gerechten Staates gelten. Dessen Vernünftigkeit muß einfach von selbst einleuchten. In diesem Sinne hat ein vernünftiges, gerechtes Staatssystem den Charakter der Ichheit. Umgekehrt gelten aus derselben Perspektive die feudalen Lebenseinrichtungen als kritisierbares Gegenbild, weil der ideologische Versuch, sie zu legitimieren, ebenso undurchsichtig für das Denken ist wie das nebelhafte Begriffsuniversum des Rationalismus. Für das selbstbewusste Denken der neuen Zeit sind somit die traditionellen Institutionen ebenso künstlich und unhaltbar wie 'the fog and illusions of an artificial world of concepts' im Rationalismus.[9]

Trotz seiner wichtigen Entdeckung läßt sich Henrich eine Unaufrichtigkeit zu schulden kommen, wenn er der klassischen, deutschen Philosophie schlechthin eine fundamentale, politische Idee von individueller Autonomie als ethisches Prinzip für den Aufbau eines modernen Staates unterstellt. Wohl hätte der junge Hegel dem Standpunkt zugestimmt, daß ein moderner, vernünftiger Staat notwendig auf einer Assoziation freier Individuen bauen muß, aber ebenso sicher hätte er individuelle Autonomie nicht als eine hinreichende Grundlage für ein wahrhaft sittliches Leben gehalten. Wie wir sehen werden, war es schon in Tübingen und Bern Hegels stillschweigender Gesichtspunkt, daß alles Leben – sowohl biologisches als menschliches – aus der Struktur einer Ganzheit begriffen werden muß. Schon bei dem jungen Hegel trat ein ausdrücklicher Vorbehalt gegenüber der radikalen Freiheitsforderung in dem Revolutionsgeist seiner Zeit auf. Philosophisch spiegelt sich dieses Problem in einer überdimensionierten Pflege des selbstbewußten Ichs auf Kosten einer schicksalshaften Ablehnung der 'contents of the world'.

Zur Charakterisierung des Deutschen Idealismus gehört also auch dieser Vorbehalt gegenüber einer radikalen Umwälzung der Gesellschaft. Die Entartung der Freiheitsideale zur terrorgefüllten Wirklichkeit in Frankreich rief Besinnung bei einigen Intellektuellen in Deutschland hervor. So basierte Schillers Aufforderung zur ästhetischen Erziehung des Menschen auf einer Vorstellung von einem harmonischen Staat, der durch in sich harmonische Individuen realisierbar ist; er forderte zu einer Beherrschung des zügellosen Freiheitsdrangs auf[10]. Ähnlich schwebte Goethe das Ideal einer menschlichen Bildung vor, in deren Prozeß die Natur das Individuum zu einem Ganzen bildet[11]. Diese erscheinungen deuteten auf einen allgemeinen Vorbehalt gegenüber Aspekten des Freiheitsbestrebens in der Zeit: Auf der einen Seite herrschte eine Zustimmung zum kritischen Aufklärungsgeist, aber auf der anderen Seite die Einsicht, daß ein wahrhaft freies Leben nur innerhalb eines vernünftigen Lebenszusammenhang möglich ist. Den historischen Studien und kritischen Schriften des jungen Hegel in Tübingen und in Bern lag diese Überzeugung von Anbeginn an zugrunde.

IV. Praktische Vernunft und sittliche Totalität

Hegels Anfänge als Schriftsteller bezeugten anscheinend einen Anschluß an Kant. In seiner Kritik an der Positivität der christlichen Religion sowie an der feudalen Machtstruktur seiner Gegenwart nahm er offenbar Kants Forderung nach einer Legitimierung durch die Vernunft in Anspruch. Um ferner an einer gesellschaftlichen Veränderung auf kultureller Ebene mitzuwirken, betrachtete er die Erziehung des einzelnen Individuums zur Mündigkeit als eine notwendige Bedingung. In den Gemütern muß praktische Vernunft erweckt werden, und insofern die Religion Liebe lehrt, unterstützt sie die Moral, denn die Liebe ist Vernunft in der Form des Gefühls. So heißt es: "Wirkung der Religion ist Verstärkung der Triebfedern der Sittlichkeit [...] und Befriedigung der Aufgaben unserer praktischen Venunft in Ansehung des [...] höchsten Guts"[12].

Darin, daß Hegel so offenbar die Religion zu einem bloßen Instrument einer aufklärerischen Volkserziehung machte, sieht Henrich eine Absage an sie zugunsten einer Wirkung individuller Autonomie[13]. Aber Henrich scheint damit zu übersehen, daß nicht diese Freiheit an sich, sondern das höchste Gut der Endzweck der Erziehung ist. Geht man diesem Endzweck richtig nach, wird man genötigt, die kantische Subjektivität im Horizonte des sozialen und gesellschaftlichen Seins zu sehen. Und dann tritt Hegels Kantianismus in ein anderes Licht. Denn demgemäß wird deutlich, daß Hegel von Anfang an – trotz seiner Benützung kantischer Terminologie – auf einen anderen Motivationskontext als Kants "Vernunft um der Vernunft willen" aus war. Die These kann belegt werden, daß der moraltheologische Aspekt von Kants Ethik eine wesentlichere Rolle als bisher angenommen spielt, ja, daß es für den jungen Hegel das Ideal eines sittlich-sozialen Ganzen in kantischer Terminologie gibt. Was Hegel erst in Frankfurt in seinen christlich-religiösen Studien als Einigkeit und Vereinigung ausdrücklich machte, wurde schon in Tübingen und Bern vorbereitet, nämlich der Gedanke, wo Kant auf dem Sittlichen als Vernunft*prinzip* besteht, es sich in Hegels – des Volkserziehers – Einstellung als Volkserzieher um die Erfüllung dieses Prinzips in *Sein* handelt. Im Gegensatz zu Kant orientierte Hegel sich an dem Sein, um überhaupt konkret verstehen zu können, was es mit dem ersten, der Vernunft, auf sich hat.

V. Die Zweideutigkeit in Hegels Kantianismus

Für Kant mußte die Ethik notwendig in eine moraltheologische Erörterung übergehen. Weil nämlich der vernünftig strebende Mensch sich mit einer unüberwindlichen Neigung behaftet erfährt, muß der verheißene Zustand von der gelingenden Vereinigung von Wollen und Wunsch als in das Jenseits projiziert und von einem allmächtigen Gott bewirkt gedacht werden. Für die Vernunft tritt dieses Konvergieren der gegensätzlichen Strebenskräfte im diesseitigen Leben als Postulat von jenseitigen Verhältnissen auf, nämlich als Freiheit, Unsterblichkeit und Gott.

Unmittelbar scheint dieser theologische Rahmen unnütz, ja sogar im Widerspruch zu Hegels Bestreben zu sein. Nur Kants Forderung nach einer Legitimierung von allen äußeren Autoritäten aus Vernunft scheint die Mündigkeit und Würde des Individuums zu fördern, weil sie die Vernunft in deren bewußtem Selbstverhältnis lokalisiert und damit eine Waffe gegen alle Positivität schafft. Nichts destoweniger legt das Prinzip individueller Autonomie nicht alles offen für eine beliebige Lebensgestaltung. Freiheit der Wahl ist nicht gemeint. Bei Kant hängen individuelle Selbstbestimmung und Wille zur sozialen Ordnung eng zusammen. Nicht nur unterdrückende Autoritäten, sondern auch beliebige Neigungen bedeuten Heteronomie des Willens, in der der Mensch sich verlieren kann. Freiheit wird somit erst in einem Leben verwirklicht, das das Gegenteil von partikulärer Gestalt hat.

Mit dieser Doppelbewegung in der Verwirklichung der Freiheit wurde Kant ein Vorbild für Hegel. Bei ihm fand er eine Begründung der Befreiung des Individuums von einem äußeren, feudalen Zwang zu einem Menschen, der nur innerhalb einer anderen sittlichen Ordnung sich selbst werden kann. So leuchtet in der wahren Autonomie eine zielrichtende Bewegung für das Leben hervor. Kants praktische Philosophie wird so das ideologische Werkzeug, dessen Hegel sich bedient in seiner Kritik an den religiösen, politischen und sozialen Verhältnissen seiner Zeit. Kants Anknüpfung an dem Selbstbewußtsein des Individuums im Handeln mußte ihm aber als beschränkt vorgekommen sein. Denn bei Kant findet das Vernunftwesen sich in seiner zugleich sinnlich-physischen Dasein gehemmt. Deshalb kehrt das Streben sich nach innen; das Gesetz wird selbstauferlegt, und Kant machte vor der eigentlichen Aufgabe einer äußeren Veränderung halt und schuf die individuelle Selbstverbesserung zum Zweck des sittlichen Strebens. Kant blieb seiner protestantischen Lebenshaltung treu, indem er hinter der Reinigung der sinnlichen Triebfedern das Ziel des Heiligkeit des Willens erblickte. Keine pragmatischen Motive dürfen sich in das Gemütsleben hineinschleichen.

Mit dem Selbstbewußtsein als Achse wurde Kant zu einer Autonomieethik geführt, die die der moralischen Handlung innewohnende Intention beschränkt. Wegen der Verbannung jedes praktischen Interesses schloß Kant sich von Gesellschaftskritik aus. Für Kant öffnet die moralische Handlungssituation eine Freiheitsperspektive im Sinne einer Möglichkeit für eine Läuterung des individuellen Charakters. Er legt die Methodenlehre der *Kritik der praktischen Vernunft* uns Vernunftwesen als Aufgabe der Selbsterziehung auf, wodurch die moralischen Maximen 'subjektiv praktisch' werden[14].

Mit diesem ethischen Individualismus ist es schwierig, Kant als die eigentliche Hintergrundfigur in Hegels religions- und kulturgeschichtlichem Engagement zu sehen. Im reinen Selbstbewußtsein ist kaum Potential zu einer Veränderung der äußeren Lebensverhältnisse. Dennoch fand Hegel bei Kant einen Ansatz zu seinem eigenen Vorhaben, und zwar in der Postulatenlehre und in der Religionsphilosophie: An die Idee des höchsten Guts, in der sich Kant die Erfüllung der moralischen Intention vorstellte, knüpfte Hegel an[15]. Nicht nur der gute Wille, sondern auch sein Effekt muß den Strebenden angehen. Kant scheint das aus dem moralisch-praktischen Handeln analytisch herzuleiten, denn dieses beabsichtigt an sich eine Veränderung[16]. Dadurch verschiebt sich die moralphilosophische Fragestellung. Das moralische Streben beabsichtigt eine Erfüllung des Guten in der Welt. Das Problem ist dann, daß die Erfüllung des Strebens der Glückseligkeit in einem Zustand des Genießens zu resultieren scheint, welcher in Kants System mit einem Rückfall in eine 'pathologische' Einstellung des Subjekts gleichbedeutend ist, die der Vernunft unterläuft. Das vernünftige Streben ist selbstverständlich gar nicht mit einer hedonistischen Einstellung vereinbar, denn die Vernunft kann nicht von selbst aus dem natürlichen Leben hervorwachsen[17]. Deshalb muß die Ethik ihre Vollendung in der Moraltheologie finden, denn die Erfüllung des Strebens kann letztendlich nur Gegenstand des Glaubens und der Hoffnung sein. Als entzweites Wesen muß der Mensch den glücklichen Zustand der Vereinigung seiner inneren Kräfte als von Gott bewirkt sehen.

Dagegen war es für den jungen Hegel von Anfang an selbstverständlich, daß es Lebensphänomene gibt, die schlechthin vernünftiger Natur sind. Die Naturreligion, die Tugenden der antiken Polis, der fromme, religiöse Mensch, sie sind alle Beispiele davon. Um für diese Fälle Platz in seinem Kantianismus zu bekommen, schien es Hegel notwendig, an die genannte Zweideutigkeit des ethischen Motivationskontextes bei Kant anzuknüpfen. Die These des Folgenden ist, daß Hegel in seinen Studien zu Volksreligion und Mythologie vorzüglich den moraltheologischen Aspekt der Kantischen Ethik im Auge hatte und dessen Idee des höchsten Guts als Vorbild für eine Vision von Sittlichkeit als möglicher, zukünftiger Realität ansah. Zuerst muß aber gezeigt werden, daß er nicht auf Kants ethisch-anthropologischer Grundlage baute, da das Individuum – wie genannt – nicht ursprünglich, sondern erst in ungünstigen Zeitverhältnissen entzweit ist.

In den *"Fragmenten über Volksreligion und Liebe"* überlegte Hegel, welche Veranstaltungen die Religion lebendig und wirksam in den Gemütern machen können, kurz: wie die Religion subjektiv werden kann. Nicht als Gesetz, sondern als lebensfördernde Macht ist die Religion für Hegel interessant. Um Innerlichkeit ging es ihm in der 'Liebe'. Deshalb ist es die Aufgabe, das gute Leben auf Liebe zu gründen. Sein Interesse spitzte sich dementsprechend zu in Richtung einer Volksreligion nach alt-griechischem Muster, die das Leben der Individuen befreien und sie in einer gemeinsamen Lebensanschauung vereinen vermag. Das Volk muß von der positiven Religion befreit werden, und durch Erziehung muß in ihnen "der göttliche Funke" erweckt werden.

Hegel meinte, eine Kraft im menschlichen Gemüt zu erblicken, die das Individuum zum "Meister über das Sinnliche" machen kann[18]. Wichtig ist aber zu betonen, daß Hegel hier nicht an die Vernunft im Sinne des kantischen Gesetzes denken kann; er richtet nämlich nicht nur sein Geschütz gegen die christliche Orthodoxie, sondern auch gegen eine Tendenz zur Fehlentwicklung, die er in dem aufklärerischen Verstandesideal sah: zu einer Pedanterie und Selbstgerechtigkeit, die mit dem schönen zwischenmenschlichen Band des Guten unverträglich ist. Die Verstandeskultur der Aufklärung fördert zwar die Mündigkeit des Einzelnen, aber kann auch die Persönlichkeit in ethischer Hinsicht verderben[19]. Deshalb muß der negativen Freiheit der Autonomie eine positive Bewegung folgen; die Vernunft muß so verstanden werden, daß sie in die Lebenseinstellung der Individuen einzugreifen vermag. Deshalb machte Hegel geschichtliche Studien, um Vorbilder für die gegenwärtige Suche nach dem guten, positiv vernünftigen Leben zu bekommen. Zu diesem Zweck berief er sich auf Kants Idee des höchsten Gutes, kleidete sie aber in ein naturalistisches

Gewand. Er wies darauf hin, daß Glückseligkeit als eine Idée der Einheit von Freiheit und Natur im *Menschen* entstanden ist, weshalb sie erfolgreich für die politische und kulturelle Bestrebungen sein kann[20].

In der griechischen Mythologie sah er das Vorbild einer sozialen Einheit in der Gestalt einer Schicksalsgemeinschaft, aber auch ein menschliches Beispiel der inneren Harmonie. Die bildliche Sprache und das Pathos der Mythen bezeugten, daß Sinnlichkeit nicht unter allen Umständen eine sittliche Ordnung anficht. Im Gegenteil, die Mythen können der Vernunft eine Leidenschaft verleihen, die sowohl "zur Äußerung des Mutes als des Lebensgenußes" reizt[21]. Das sinnliche Element der Mythen droht nicht der Vernunft, sondern verleiht dem moralischen Streben mit einer zusätzlichen Motivation zu gemeinschaftlichem Handeln.

Damit schienen Hegels Studien zur Antike von einem ähnlichen Motiv getrieben zu sein wie – auf andere Weise zwar – Kant in seiner Postulatenlehre; nämlich von der Absicht, der Schwächung beizukommen, die eintritt, wenn Glückseligkeit nicht als Anregung gelten darf[22]. Hegels naturalistische Umdeutung von Kants Moraltheologie bestätigt sich auch darin, daß er durchgehend den griechischen Fatalismus dem christlichen Jenseitsglauben vorzieht: Nicht auf Ersatz im Jenseits für erlittene Schmerzen im Diesseits zu hoffen, sondern die Menschen zur Übernahme des Lebens im Guten und Schlechten zu erziehen.

VI. Idealisierung der Natur. Der Ansatz bei Kant

Gegen Henrichs Auffassung scheint vieles dafür zu sprechen, daß Hegels Interesse an der Verwirklichung der der wahren Religion innewohnenden Ethik mit einer Anknüpfung an Kants Moraltheologie verbunden ist: Er nimmt Kants Idee des höchsten Gutes in Anspruch zu einem Aufbau einer griechisch inspirierten Sittlichkeit, die sich an der Vorstellung von einem Gemeinschaftsleben orientieren soll. Zu dem Zweck muß er aber ein Hindernis in dem anthropologischen Fundament bei Kant loswerden; er muß sich mit seinem Naturbegriff auseinandersetzen.

Kant hatte selbst angefangen, einen versöhnenden Klang in seine rigoristische Ethik zu bringen. Er wollte zeigen, daß die Welt so beschaffen ist, daß ihre Entwicklung der moralischen Absicht des Individuums entgegenkommt. So stellte er Gott vor als "eine oberste Ursache der Natur […], die einer der moralischen Gesinnung gemäße Kausalität hat"[23]. Wie schon in der "Methodenlehre" der *Kritik der reinen Vernunft* dargelegt, so forderte die Vorstellung von der Glückseligkeit der Menschen eine sogenannte physikotheologische Revision der Naturwissenschaften, deren zufolge "die Welt als aus einer Idee entsprungen vorgestellt werden muß", weshalb "dem Naturforschen eine Richtung nach der Form eines Systems der Zwecke" gegeben werden muß[24].

Nun scheint Hegel in seinen historischen Studien nicht ausdrücklich von Kant angeregt zu sein, aber zweifellos entspricht der organische Zug in Kants moralischem Weltbegriff der Idee einer Einheit von Vernunft und Natur, die Hegel im griechischen Polisleben verwirklicht sah. 'Volksreligion' bedeutet bei Hegel die ethisch vorbildhafte Zusammenschmelzung von Vernunft und Natur. Noch wichtiger ist, daß Kants physikotheologischer Grundgedanke das Fundament für eine Anthropologie sein könnte, die für Hegels Vorhaben günstig wäre: Bewußtsein des Gesetzes und Kraft der Sinnlichkeit könnten als ursprünglich Eines in der menschlichen Natur gedacht werden. Engagement und Einheit des öffentlichen Lebens, die Hegel als Volkserzieher gerne sah, ist nur möglich, wenn das menschliche Individuum trotz seines entzweiten Daseins im Grunde einheitlich beschaffen ist.

Hegels Subjektivierung der Religion zielt darauf hin, einen Gegenzug zur abstrakten Verstandesaufklärung zu sein mit dem "lebendigen Buch der Natur"[25] als Vorbild. Entsprechend dürfen die sozialen Einrichtungen kein Kabinett von toten Individuen sein, so wie der Verstand sie sieht. Im Gegenteil, daß Hegel der Religion einen erhabeneren Schwung geben möchte, bedeutet, daß ihre Ethik dem Leben dienen soll und "eine unendliche Mannigfaltigkeit von Zwecken zu einem freundschaftlichen Band knüpfen" kann.[26]

In diesem Punkte entspricht sein Vorhaben eigentlich Kierkegaards Subjektivitäts-Dictum. Wie Kierkegaard die Aufgabe der subjektiven Aneignung im Christentum wiederentdeckte und gegen das System des späten Hegel geltend machen wollte, so klagte der junge Hegel mit seiner subjektiven Religion den Aufklärungsverstand und die Dogmatik wegen Lebensfeindlichkeit an. Nur vertrat der junge Hegel ein soziales Lebensideal, wo Kierkegaard hingegen auf der Innerlichkeit und individuellen Exklusivität der Gottesbeziehung beharrt. Dagegen soll Hegels Religion positiv-organisch auf den ganzen menschlichen Charakter wirken und den Willen zum Guten fördern, ihr den Charakter eines unterdrückenden Gesetzes nehmen[27] und stattdessen eine Öffnung zu einem Leben mit dem Mitmenschen sein.

Für Hegel ist es die wichtigste Funktion der Religion, die Entfaltung des ganzen Menschen zu bewirken in einer bejahenden Teilnahme am Leben der sozialen und kulturellen Ganzheit. Die Ordnung, die Kant in der selbstbewußten, praktischen Vernunft zu sehen meinte, begann Hegel allmählich in den antiken Tugenden und letztendlich in einer mythologisch geschauten Lebensganzheit verwirklicht zu sehen. So spricht viel dafür, daß die Grundzüge von Hegels moralphilosophischer Position schon in Tübingen und Bern festlagen. Nicht so sehr um individuelle Freiheit sondern um eine soziale – ästhetisch unterbaute – Erfüllung der Bedingungen eines Lebens in der Gemeinschaft ging es.

Henrich führt an, daß Hegel sich an Kants Modernisierung des Christentums, die auf Autonomie ohne Gott und Unsterblichkeit angelegt war, angeschlossen hatte. Theologische Metaphysik spielte eine untergeordnete Rolle. Zwar waren die Griechen Hegels Vorbilder, aber nur wegen eines geschichtlichen Glückfalls konnte damals ihre Freiheit sich als "harmonisches, öffentliches Leben" entfalten. Unter unglücklichen Bedingungen wie den zu Hegels Zeit mußte die Freiheit sich dagegen in der Gestalt der inneren Unabhängigkeit finden.

Dieser Gesichtspunkt gibt Anlaß zur Verwunderung. Hegel in Bern als modernen kantianischen Freiheitsphilosophen anzusehen, scheint nicht berechtigt zu sein. Hatte der junge Hegel nicht eben begeistert die Antike als Exponent eines höheren Freiheitsgeistes gerühmt und die moderne Aufklärung abgewertet, dessen Verstand die Natur verbildet? Sicherlich aber verfügte Hegel damals noch nicht über eine geschichtsphilosophische Konzeption, die den modernen individualistischen Freiheitsbegriff in ein versöhnendes Licht rücken, und die die antike Idee einer Lebensgemeinschaft als relativ berechtigt innerhalb einer Theorie, die die moderne Autonomie bevorzugt, hervorscheinen lassen könnte.

Für Henrichs Interpretation könnte indessen Hegels Begeisterung für Fichtes revolutionären Geist als eine Zustimmung zu dem modernen Emanzipationsideal in Anspruch genommen werden[28]. Hegel rühmt die Griechen dafür, daß sie ihre Freiheit durch einen Befreiungskampf gewonnen hatten, aber nicht, um einen politischen Individualismus zu verwirklichen. Um auf die richtige Spur zu kommen, muß der theologischen Metaphysik eine gewisse Rolle eingeräumt werden. In Kants Physikotheologie sah Hegel in Bern eine naturphilosophisch basierte Idee von einer vollkommenen Ordnung in der Welt. Er wollte Kants "legitimierte Idee von Gott jetzt rückwärts brauchen […] in Erklärung der Zweckbeziehung", d.h. den Gottesbegriff politisch-philosophisch zu einer Vision von einem zukünftigen Zustand gebrauchen, der dem individuellen moralischen Streben entgegenkommen würde[29]. Mit dieser Vision hatte er implizit mit Kants Autonomieethik gebrochen. Eine neue philosophische Anthropologie scheint unumgänglich; er muß mit dem Gedanken einer ursprünglichen Einheit von Vernunft und Natur ansetzen, demzufolge ein Streben als vernünftig angesehen wird, wenn es die Autonomie des *ganzen* Menschen und nicht nur der Vernunft fördert.

Hegel suchte früh einen Punkt, in dem Vernunft und Natur zusammentreffen. Das bezeugt seine metaphorische Rede von dem Licht, das nicht rein, sondern nur indirekt in Farben als ihrem Anderssein sichtbar wird, und von dem Salz, wenn es nicht als Klumpen isoliert, sondern als aufgelöst das Wasser durchdringt und als Salziges allgegenwärtig wird. Ähnlich sind die Ideen von Freiheit und Vernunft isoliert gesehen bloß Abstraktionen und nur in ihrem 'Anderssein' wirklich, d.a. in ihrer Prägung von der seelischen Ganzheit[30].

So scheint Hegel eher an Rousseau als an Kant anzuknüpfen, wenn er von dem 'Subjektiven' als von "aus der Moralität hervorgehenden Empfindungen"[31] spricht. In den 'Empfindungen' scheint Hegel das Gesuchte zu finden, nämlich einen Punkt in der intersubjektiven Beziehung, der als tätige Empfänglichkeit für den anderen Menschen die Gegenüberstellung von aktiver Vernunft und passiver Neigung im Bewußtsein zu vermeiden scheint. Für Kant konnte Intersubjektivität nicht als Ansatz der Ethik dienen, weil sie mit einem Moment der Sinnlichkeit behaftet ist, die zu sehr mit der Neigung verbunden ist. Dagegen meinte Hegel in der empfindenden Einstellung der Offenheit für den Anderen, kurz: in der Liebe, ein einheitliches Phänomen zu sehen, die der kantischen Dichotomie unterläuft. Phänomene wie Mitleid, Freundschaft, Wohlwollen scheinen ursprünglich, i.e. nicht einer Teilung in Vernunft und Neigung fähig zu sein, weshalb sie nicht schlechthin als pathologisch beurteilt werden können. So wagte Hegel, sich der Natur anzunähern, weil sie nicht immer Heteronomie des Willens bedeutet. Im Gegenteil hielt er als das Grundprinzip des empirischen Charakters die Liebe, "die etwas Analoges mit der Vernunft hat, insofern sie in anderen Menschen sich selbst findet oder vielmehr sich selbst vergessend sich aus seiner Existenz heraussetzt, gleichsam in anderen lebt, empfindet und tätig ist – so wie die Vernunft, als Prinzip allgemeingeltender Gesetze, sich selbst wieder in jedem vernünftigen Wesen erkennt […]"[32].

Bei Kant tauchte die Vernunft im Selbstbewußtsein als Gesetz auf; hingegen meinte Hegel, in der Liebe die Allgemeinheit der Vernunft in der Gestalt einer Kraft zu sehen, die die zwischenmenschlichen Schranken niederreißt und ein gemeinsames Leben ermöglicht. Dadurch scheint er, die Beschränktheit, die

die unvermittelte Autonomie sich selbst setzt, überwunden zu haben, nämlich zu sich selbst ohne durch den Anderen kommen zu wollen. Kurz: Schon hier formulierte Hegel die Einsicht, mit der er später dem Problem der autonomen Freiheit, den Anderen als Grenze zu erfahren, beikam. Hiermit war so der intersubjektive Ansatz gegründet, den Hegel später in Frankfurt unter Hölderlins Einfluß voll entwickelte. Jetzt aber hatte er sich – mit der griechischen Mythologie und der christlichen Nächstenliebe in seinen Gedanken – den Weg zu einer moralphilosophischen Position gebahnt, die sich aus der Idee der Selbstverwirklichung in Beziehung zum Anderen und zur Lebensganzheit orientierte. Um den realen Kontext von diesem neuen Sittlichkeitskonzept deutlicher zu entfalten, können Lukács' Untersuchungen mit Vorteil einbezogen werden.

VII. Das republikanische Ideal. Georg Lukács

Schon in Tübingen hob Hegel den Geist des antiken, griechischen Staates als Vorbild eines sittlichen Lebens hervor. In seinen historischen und politischen Studien hatte er die Griechen für ihre vorbildhafte Auffassung von der Beziehung zwischen Individuum und Gemeinschaft gerühmt: Bei ihnen bezeichnete Gemeinschaft nicht eine Begrenzung sondern die Erfüllung der Freiheit des Einzelnen. In dem Fragment *"Die Positivität der christlichen Religion"* bevorzugt er die sokratische Weisheit vor dem in Jesus personifizierten moralischen Ideal. Lieber Selbstständigkeit im Sinne von allseitiger Entwicklung von menschlichen Kräften und Fähigkeiten als Abhängigkeit von einem unerreichbaren übermenschlichen Beispiel.

Wichtig ist hier, daß Hegel die sokratische Methode als einen Ausdruck der politischen Gesinnung der antiken Polis sieht. Die Freunde von Sokrates hätten "republikanischen Geist eingesogen"[33], während die urchristliche Gemeinde ganz und gar "an einer Person gehängt" habe. Hegels Zustimmung zu Sokrates liegt so folgende Auffassung zugrunde: Ethische Weisheit ist Ausdruck einer menschlichen Vollkommenheit, die auf Selbstständigkeit gründet, und diese wird nur unter Verhältnissen erreicht, die so beschaffen sind, daß sie die Selbstentfaltung des ganzen Menschen in einem sozialen Zusammenhang fördern. Bei den Griechen spürt Hegel also eine Idee von einer Lebensganzheit, aus deren Perspektive die Idee eines erfüllten sittlichen Lebens erblickt werden kann. Nicht von der Stimme der Vernunft im Selbstbewußtsein, sondern aus dem Geist einer wahren Gemeinschaft soll gelernt werden, was die Freiheit in concreto ist. Deshalb geht das republikanische Leben die Ethik an.

Es ist der Verdienst von Georg Lukács, in seinen Untersuchungen zum jungen Hegel gezeigt zu haben, daß das politische und soziale Leben ein zentrales Motiv im Denken des jungen Hegel war, wenn es um die Idee der sittlichen Selbstverwirklichung geht[34]. Lukács verschärft seine politisch-philosophische Pointe durch den Nachweis, daß Hegels Studien zum griechischen Altertum von dem Gedanken geleitet sind, daß ein öffentliches gemeinsames Leben befreiende Züge besitzt und deshalb wesentlich für eine Ethik ist, die an einem Begriff der Freiheit orientiert ist. Die nahe Beziehung von individueller Freiheit und Politik legt Lukács seinen Untersuchungen zugrunde und hebt Hegels Gesichtspunkt hervor, daß Freiheit in modernen kapitalistischen Gesellschaften als Autonomie aufgefaßt wird, weil diese Gesellschaften keinen positiven Anknüpfungspunkt für die Sehnsucht des Einzelnen nach einer wahren Gemeinschaft zu liefern vermögen. Anders als beim späten Hegel spürt man bei dem jungen Hegel einen geschichtsphilosophischen Pessimismus, demzufolge mit der Spätantike eine Fragmentierung der Gesellschaft, die auch noch die Moderne prägt, einsetze: "Das Bild des Staates als ein Produkt seiner Tätigkeit verschwand aus der Seele des Bürgers" – und überließ ihm nur einen Teil "des zerstückelten Ganzen"[35].

Lukács charakterisiert Hegels Ideal einer Republik als eine politische Gemeinschaft von kollektiver Selbstbestimmung, als eine Ganzheit, die immer wieder von ihren Mitgliedern geschaffen und aufrechterhalten wird, und die sich deshalb nicht zu einer mechanischen Staatsmaschine gegenüber den Bürgern verselbständigt hat. Hegel konnte die republikanischen Tugenden hervorheben und von Hingebung und Aufopferung für das Vaterland sprechen, weil die höhere Ordnung des Staates in der antiken Polis kein System von festgelegten Institutionen war, sondern in der Einigkeit der kollektiven Selbstgesetzgebung und Selbstverwaltung[36] bestand. Als entscheidend für Hegel hebt er "das Nicht-für-immer-Festgelegte der Objektivität [...], die Richtung zum Objektiven und von dort wieder zurück in die geänderte, geläuterte Subjektivität" hervor als das Freiheitsmoment im antiken politischen Leben.

Lukács behauptet mit Recht, daß Hegels zwar idealisierte Vorstellung von der antiken Polis nicht ganz und gar ein romantisches Kontrastbild zu seiner Gegenwart oder ein Anachronismus war. Im Gegenteil, es ging eine direkte Linie von dem sozialen Ideal bei den Griechen zu den – von Hegel weithin angeeigneten – Idealen der Französischen Revolution: Demokratie, soziale und ökonomische Gleichheit.

Die geschichtsphilosophische Perspektive, aus der der junge Hegel mehr oder weniger explizit seine Gegenwart beurteilte, bezeugt, daß der Begriff von Freiheit als individueller Selbstbestimmung in der Privatsphäre – als Autonomie – nur ein schlechter Ersatz von einem höheren, universellen Begriff von Freiheit als Selbstverwirklichung in einem politischen Zusammenhang ist. Also scheint Henrich mit seiner autonomie-ethischen Interpretation von Hegels Studien in Bern und Tübingen die Untersuchungen Lukács' nicht überbieten zu können. Es ist immer noch dessen Verdienst, gezeigt zu haben, daß Hegel unter Freiheit mehr als ein individuelles Selbstverhältnis verstand; daß also nicht nur Kants Begriff von praktischer Vernunft ihm am Herzen lag, sondern der Gedanke von einem harmonischen Ganzen, an dessen Leben wahre Freiheit verwirklicht ist. Im Gesellschaftsleben waltet Freiheit nicht nur, weil individuelle Bedürfnisse befriedigt werden, sondern weil es schlechthin das Zentrum der Verwirklichung von allen menschlichen Bedürfnissen, Kräften und Fähigkeiten in einer Gemeinsamkeit ist.

Folglich bedeutet Hegels Kantianismus keine Zustimmung zum Individualismus im kantischen Sinne; in Kants Vernunftbegriff sah Hegel die Achtung vor der Würde des Individuums wegen dessen Fähigkeit zur Autonomie[37], aber diese Würde nahm er nur im Anspruch, um wider die Ortodoxie zu behaupten, daß der Mensch von Natur aus gut ist; dieser Gesichtspunkt ist die erste Bedingung für die Möglichkeit einer Idee von Sittlichkeit als Leben und nicht nur als Gesinnung.

VIII. Republikanische Metaphysik. Wilhelm Dilthey

Ihren Verdiensten zum Trotz leiden Lukács' Untersuchungen zum jungen Hegel an den Reduktionen des historischen Materialismus. So meint Lukács zu wissen, daß das Kernstück der Ethik bei dem jungen Hegel – die Religion – bloß ideologischer Schein sei. In Wirklichkeit zeichneten Hegels Studien sich durch ein angebliches Grundstreben aus, "die wirkliche innere Struktur, die wirklichen treibenden Kräfte seiner Gegenwart, des Kapitalismus gedanklich zu erfassen, die Dialektik zu begründen"[38]. Aber trotz dieser ideologisch motivierten Reduktion von Hegels Anliegen weist Lukács auf eine wichtige Sphäre von Hegels Ethik hin, die mit dem kantischen individualistischen Rahmen aber unverträglich ist.

Dagegen scheinen Diltheys Untersuchungen zum jungen Hegel nicht an solcher Reduktion zu leiden, und zudem hält er – wie Lukács – an Hegels ganzheitlicher Orientierung fest. Mit Blick auf den spinozistischen Einschlag in der ersten nachkantischen Generation nennt er Hegel einen der Urheber des modernen Pantheismus[39]. Trotzdem widersteht Dilthey Lukács' Vorwurf, er unterstelle Hegel einen "romantischen Tiefsinn". Dilthey unterstreicht, daß die Gedanken des jungen Hegel von Anfang an tief in den Idealen der modernen Aufklärung verwurzelt waren und daß die politische Freiheit der altgriechischen Staaten genau die Existenzgrundlage ihrer bewundernswerten Humanität war.

Wollen wir Hegels Idee der Lebensganzheit aus ihrer gesellschaftlichen Einkleidung herauskristallisieren, können wir uns besonders an Dilthey wenden. Ihm zufolge ist sie in Hegels "pantheistischer Weltanschauung" in seinem Gedicht an Hölderlin ausgesprochen. Das Gedicht über den Einweihungsgang der eleusischen Mysterien gibt zu erkennen, daß die pantheistische Strömung von Plato bis Spinoza die beiden Freunde schon zu ihrer Studentenzeit in Tübingen beeinflußt hat[40]. Nicht so sehr subjektzentrierte Vernunftkritik, sondern eine Metaphysik der Lebensganzheit, die auf das kritische Vorhaben der kantischen Philosophie versöhnend reagieren sollte, war das gemeinsame Anliegen der beiden Freunde von Anfang an. Aber wie kann Dilthey die Beziehung von Pantheismus und empirischer, politischer Wirklichkeit dann näher aufweisen? Welche Erfahrung gibt der Pantheismus, die auf die sittliche Realität Einfluß haben kann?

Metaphysisch gestimmt ist der Text mit Recht nur als Gedicht; im Zusammenhang mit Hegels realitätsbezogenen historischen und politischen Studien ist seine Relevanz dagegen schwieriger aufzuweisen. Näher betrachtet sieht Hegel in dem eleusischen Einweihungsgang eine Doppelbewegung, in der die Selbstveräußerung in der Hingebung an das Unendliche, Unermeßliche (*'hen kai pan'*) in einem mit der gegenläufigen Bewegung geht, sich wieder in erneuter konkreter Gestalt zu empfangen. Und darin bestand – so Hegel – die sittliche Weisheit der Griechen: Es ging ihnen darum, das Private ("was mein ich nannte")[41] los zu werden, und das vermochte nur die Hingebung zum Unendlichen, die die Idee des Kosmos nährte und dadurch das spezifisch griechische Zentrum der sittlichen Orientierung erschuf. Nicht aus selbstbewußter Vernunft, sondern direkt aus den Taten und Leben der Griechen offenbart sich diese Weisheit. Dilthey setzt deshalb zu Recht die Mysterienweisheit der Griechen mit ihrem politischen Leben in Verbindung, wenn er von ihr behauptet: "Die Vision endet in dem Ideal, das ihn [Hegel] zu dieser Zeit ganz erfüllte. Den Griechen erschien das Geheimnis des Unendlichen in der idealen sittlichen Ordnung ihres Staats und nicht nur in Worten"[42].

So ist Lukács' Behauptung, daß Dilthey Hegels Jugendschriften in eine irrationalistische, lebensphilosophische Richtung[43] verfälscht habe, weil er die Bedeutung der materiellen und politischen Wirklichkeit ignoriert, bodenlos. Im Gegenteil, in Diltheys Untersuchungen hat Lukács selbst einen ausdrücklichen Beleg für seinen eigenen Gesichtspunkt finden können, nämlich daß Staat und Sittlichkeit von zentraler Bedeutung für Hegel waren. Der Verdienst von Lukács besteht darin, Hegels Blick für die sozialen, politischen und materiellen Aspekte der sittlichen Frage aufgezeigt zu haben. Dilthey aber pointiert mit ebenso großem Recht die konstitutive Bedeutung der idealistischen Metaphysik für den griechischen Republikaner, – nämlich daß der Gedanke des Kosmos, der Sinn für das Einheitliche, Harmonische eben in der politischen Tätigkeit der Griechen als Idee wirksam war. Politische Akteure prägen ihre gesellschaftliche Wirklichkeit mit ihren Vorstellungen; deshalb hat Dilthey recht, wenn er die Bedeutung von Hegels pantheistischer Metaphysik hervorhebt. Den Griechen – und auch Hegel – würde Lukács' Gesichtspunkt nicht gefallen, da er die Erkenntnis nur für "die gedanklichen Spiegelbilder jener Dialektik, die sich objektiv, unabhängig von Wissen und Willen der Menschen in ihrem Leben abspielt", ansieht[44]. Mit 'Eleusis' kommen wir dagegen auf die Spur der Metaphysik, die später in Hegels Denken immer ausdrücklicheres Interesse findet als Grundlage von Systematisierungsversuchen, die 'Vereinigung', 'Leben' und 'Geist' als Schlüsselwörter haben.

IX. Konklusion

Wie die vorhergehenden Untersuchungen zeigen sollten, übersieht Dieter Henrich wichtige Motive in Hegels Tübinger und Berner Studien zur Sittlichkeit. Zwar betont er mit Recht die Anwesenheit von Kants Theorie der praktischen Vernunft in Hegels Denken zu dieser Zeit, aber er übersieht, daß Hegels Vorgänger nur ein Moment lieferte; daß Sittlichkeit aber nicht nur ein subjektives Vermögen ist, sondern wesentlich darin besteht, den Ethos eines gemeinschaftlichen Lebens zu besitzen. Henrich scheint außerdem Hölderlins Einfluß auf Hegels Denken zu übertreiben: "Daß die griechische Politie Vereinigung, nicht nur Verbindung der Freien gewesen sei, daß Freiheit nicht nur als Selbstheit, […] als Achtung fürs Moralgesetz sei"[45] – wußte nicht nur Hölderlin; mit dieser Einsicht war Hegel schon vertraut, ehe er 1797 nach Frankfurt kam.

So spricht mehreres dafür, daß Hegel Hölderlins Idee der Vereinigung nur als ein begriffliches Werkzeug übernahm, weil sie seine eigene sittliche Vision in den gegenwärtigen, philosophischen Zusammenhang überführen und prägnanter zum Ausdruck bringen konnte. Er brauchte die Inspiration von seinem Freund, um seinen Gedanken begriffliche Schärfe geben zu können. Hegel war also nie eindeutiger Kantianer. Wenn es so aussehen könnte, hängt das nur damit zusammen, daß Hegel in Bern und Tübingen nicht eigentlich Philosoph war; Kant figurierte überall in seinen frühen Schriften, einfach weil seine praktische Philosophie die besten zeitgemäßen begrifflichen Mittel zur Verfügung für Hegels Vorhaben stellte. Hegel gehörte aber von Anfang an zu der objektiv-idealistischen Reaktion auf Kant, die sich auf die pantheistische Strömung von Platon bis Spinoza berief. Innerhalb ihrer interessierte es ihn, die metaphysische Idee des Ganzen als sittliche Totalität, als ein soziales gesellschaftliches Leben auszulegen.[46]

Anmerkungen
1. In der Schrift *Differenz des fichteschen und schellingschen Systems der Philosophie* 1801.
2. Henrich, Dieter (1971).
3. Bondeli, Martin (1997).
4. Dilthey, Wilhelm (1968).
5. Henrich (1971) 22 f.
6. Ibid. 24.
7. Henrich (1992) 94.
8. Ibid. 84.
9. Ibid.
10. Schiller, Friedrich *Über die äesthetische Erziehung des Menschen.*
11. Goethe *Wilhelm Meisters Lehrjahre.*
12. Hegel (1970) 1, 88.
13. Henrich (1971) 51.
14. Kant, Immanuel (1985) 237.
15. Er überlegt die Möglichkeit einer Legitimierung der Gottesidee, um die Folgen des moralischen Strebens darzulegen. Vgl. *Briefe I*, 17.
16. "... weil das moralische Gesetz will, daß das höchste durch uns mögliche Gut bewirkt werde ...". Kant (1990) 6.
17. "Die völlige Angemessenheit des Willens [...] zum Gesetz ist Heilligkeit, eine Vollkommenheit, deren kein vernünftiges Wesen der Sinnenwelt in keinem Zeitpunkt seines Daseins fähig ist". Kant (1985).
18. Hegel (1970) I, 96.
19. Vgl. Hegel (1970) I, 21, 26.
20. Hegel (1970) I, 97.
21. Hegel (1970) I, 17.
22. Vgl. Henrich (1971) 48 ff.
23. Kant (1985) 144.
24. Vgl. Kant (1956) 736.
25. Hegel (1970) I, 14.

26. Ibid.
27. Vgl. Hegel (1970) I, 17.
28. Vgl. Hegel (1953) I, 16,18.
29. Op.cit. I, 17.
30. Hegel (1970) I, 11.
31. Hegel (1970) I, 15. Über Rousseaus Einfluß auf den jungen Hegel, siehe Henrich (1971) 44.
32. Hegel (1970) I, 30.
33. Vgl. I, 120.
34. Lukács (1973).
35. I, 206.
36. Vgl. Hegel (1970) I, 205: "Als freie Menschen gehorchten sie Gesetzen, die sie sich selbst gegeben [...]". Lukács (1973): I, 101.
37. Hegel meint: die Vernunft zur Autonomie entwickelt gibt dem Individuum die Stärke der Ganzheitlichkeit. Vgl. (1970) I, 96.
38. Lukács (1973) I, 27.
39. Vgl. Dilthey (1968) Bd. XV ("Rezension") 311-312.
40. Daß die Erinnerung an den Bund der beiden Freunde mit dem Hingebung an das Unendliche und Unermeßliche verbunden zu sein scheint.
41. Hegel (1970) I, 231.
42. Dilthey 4, 39.
43. vgl. Lukács (1973) 13-15.
44. Lukács I, 31.
45. Henrich (1971) 24.

Literaturverzeichnis

Dilthey, Wilhelm (1968) "Die Jugendgeschichte Hegels" *Gesammelte Schriften Bd. 4* (Stuttgart. Teubner).
Bondeli, Martin (1997) *Der Kantianismus des jungen Hegels* (Hamburg, Felix Meiner).
Hegel, Georg Wilhelm Friedrich (1970) Werke 1-20. (Frankfurt m Main, Suhrkamp Verlag) 1, 88.
Hegel, Georg Wilhelm Friedrich (1953) briefe von und an Hegel 1-4.
Henrich, Dieter (1971) *Hegel im Kontext* (Frankfurt am Main, Suhrkamp Verlag).
Henrich, Dieter (1992) "The french Revolution and Classical German Philosophy", *Aesthetic Judgement and the moral Image of the World. Studies in Kant* (Stanford, California).
Kant, Immanuel (1985) *Kritik der praktischen Vernunft* (Hamburg, Felix Meiner).
Kant, Immanuel (1956) *Kritik der reinen Vernunft* (Hamburg, Felix Meiner).
Kant, Immanuel (1990) *Die Religion inderhalb der Grenzen der bloßen Vernunft* (Hamburg, Felix Meiner).
Lukács, Georg (1973) *Der junge Hegel I-II* (Ulm, Suhrkamp).

PRIVILEGED ACCESS AND TWO KINDS OF SEMANTIC EXTERNALISM

JESPER KALLESTRUP

Department of Philosophy
University of Copenhagen

1. The MC-form

Semantic externalism is standardly taken as the thesis that the contents of intentional states fail to supervene on intrinsic, physical properties of individuals, but instead depend for their individuation on the physical nature of their environment. My Earthly tokens of 'water' pick out H_2O, but on Twin Earth my doppelgänger's tokens of 'water' pick out XYZ. But meaning determines reference, so I express the concept <water>, whereas my doppelgänger expresses the concept <twin-water>.[1] The lesson that certain semantic properties are relational, carries over to the corresponding intentional properties. We are in different wide belief states given that such states are partly individuated by their contents: I believe that water is wet, but he believes that twin-water is wet.[2]

Equally well-known is the Privileged Access thesis: a competent thinker can have a priori knowledge of the intentional and semantic properties of the contents of her own occurrent thoughts. In the normal run of things, I can thus know a priori that I am thinking that water is wet if I am. This is reflected by an asymmetry in psychological discourse between first-person and third-person utterances. A sincere and competent first-person avowal that one is in a basic mental state is taken to be authoritative in the sense that such a claim is justified without one being required to adduce grounds to support it. In contrast, a third-person observer cannot justifiably assert that one is in a mental state without producing grounds provided by inference from one's behaviour.[3]

It is widely acknowledged, as in Davidson (1987) and Burge (1988), that there is a *prima facie* tension between semantic externalism and Privileged Access. It is easy to see the worry. How can we be authoritative about the occurrent contents of our own minds if, as semantic externalism tells us, those contents depend for their individuation on circumstances that we have no special authority about, or may even lack knowledge of? It is, however, worth trying to bring out this apparent tension in a more cogent fashion. One way of doing that is a *reductio* of the following MC-form; cf. McKinsey (1991), Boghossian (1997), McLaughlin & Tye (1998), Davies (1998):

(1) I have mental property M,
(2) If I have mental property M, then I meet condition C,
(3) So, I meet condition C,

where C is an external proposition that makes M a wide state. For instance, if M is the state I am in when I think that water is wet, then C is the proposition that I, or members of my speech community, sustain causal connections with water, or just that water exists. Now, (1) is a priori knowable by Privileged Access, and (2) is a conceptual truth, so a priori knowable, according to semantic externalism. Hence, (3) can be deduced on purely a priori grounds, and therefore can itself be known a priori.[4] Yet this is incredible since C embraces propositions about ordinary empirical states of affairs of which, intuitively at least, I have no a priori access. I cannot know a priori that I have interacted with water or even that water exists.[5]

It may be objected that (2) is insufficiently supported by the Twin Earth argument. As the contra-positive makes clear, it is not enough to show that certain contents of intentional states depend for their individuation on the nature of their physical environment. What must be shown is, moreover, that such contents depend for their existence on the existence of appropriate objects in that environment. And clearly all the Twin Earth argument shows, if good, is that natural kind concepts are externally individuated. But to sustain the a priority of (2), it has to be shown a priori that the very existence of such concepts is dependent upon the existence of an extension.

Boghossian (1998, p. 255) has argued that such warrant is forthcoming once we consider Dry Earth on which, despite all appearances, there is neither water nor twin-water:

> "If there is no kind denoted by a given natural kind term – say, 'water' – then no satisfaction conditions for that term will have been pinned down. The actual kind of stuff at the end of the relevant causal chain is supposed to fix the kind of stuff that is denoted by 'water'. If there's nothing there, then, it would seem, there is no fact of the matter what kind of stuff there would have to be for the extension of the term not to be empty."

So, not only are all tokens of 'water' empty on Dry Earth, there are not even conditions, following semantic externalism, under which they would not have been empty, but that is just to say that such tokens fail to express a concept. Why is the semantic externalist forced to say that natural kind concepts are *ob-*

ject-dependent in this manner given what she says about Twin Earth? The train of thought seems to be that if the individuation of the concept expressed by 'water' is indifferent to the existence of water, then it should also be indifferent to the substitution of water for twin-water. But since it is not indifferent to the substitution of water for twin-water, neither is it indifferent to the existence of water.

Suppose for the moment that Boghossian's argument is sound. Then we seem to have a *reductio* of compatibilism, i.e. the view that Privileged Access is consistent with semantic externalism. Most semantic externalists, e.g. Burge (1988), Davidson (1987), McLaughlin & Tye (1998), agree that if we have a *reductio* of compatibilism, then we also have something very close to a *reductio* of semantic externalism. They have therefore spent much energy combating incompatibilist arguments. I shall argue in the following that instances of the MC-form do show that we have a *reductio* of compatibilism, but only given a strong form of semantic externalism. If, however, we settle for a weaker form of semantic externalism, then we need not fear the MC-form.

2. Descriptivism and Referentialism

Many philosophers agree that there is a close connection between, on the one hand, semantic internalism and descriptivism – the view that a term N has associated with it a set of descriptive properties f as its propositional content such that an object o is picked out by N iff o has f; where the propositional content of a term is its contribution to determine the proposition expressed by sentences containing it. Thus suppose 'water' is associated with the property of being the watery stuff, i.e. the clear, potable liquid that falls from the sky, etc. On this account, my utterance of 'water is wet' has *descriptive truth-conditions*: it is true iff the watery stuff is wet. But these are also the conditions under which my doppelgänger's utterance of the same sentence is true. After all, twin-water shares the superficial, watery properties with water, and my doppelgänger and I both associate these properties with 'water'. If we identity propositions with truth-conditions, then by sentences containing 'water', I express *descriptive propositions* containing the descriptive concept <the watery stuff>, but so does my doppelgänger on Twin Earth. It follows that supervenience holds, and therefore that we are in the same narrow mental states: we both believe that the watery stuff is wet.

On the other hand, there is also a close connection between semantic externalism and referentialism – the view that the only semantic function N has is to refer to o such that the propositional content of N is given by o itself and not by any associated descriptive properties. On this account, my utterance of 'water is wet' has *singular truth-conditions*: it is true iff water, i.e. H_2O, is wet. By utterances of sentences containing 'water', I express *singular propositions* which are partially constituted by water itself. But my doppelgänger's utterance on Twin Earth of 'water is wet' has different singular truth-conditions: it is true iff twin-water, i.e. XYZ, is wet. By utterances of sentences containing 'water', my doppelgänger express singular propositions which in part contain twin-water itself. My doppelgänger causally interacts with twin-water, and so cannot use 'water' to express the singular concept <water>. It follows that supervenience fails, and that we therefore are in different wide mental states: I believe that water is wet, but my doppelgänger believes that twin-water is wet.

Now, semantic internalism is clearly an implausible view if it goes hand-in-hand with this form of descriptivism. There is a widespread intuition that even though the inhabitants on Twin Earth call XYZ 'water', we should not. Water is all and only H_2O. Maybe we should therefore opt for the combination of referentialism and semantic externalism instead. But this by-passes an obvious hybrid construction. One can remain a semantic externalist and yet hang on to descriptivism if only one builds certain *indexical* properties into the descriptive content of referring terms. Thus suppose 'water' expresses the causally constrained, descriptive concept <the watery stuff of our acquaintance>. Then my use of 'water' does not pick out XYZ on Twin Earth, because XYZ is not the watery stuff with which I am acquainted.[6] Importantly, my doppelgänger and I will associate the same causal property with 'water', i.e. the property of being acquainted with a watery stuff, but, as Lewis (1979) emphasised, the truth-conditions of our utterances will be different. My utterance of 'water is wet' is true iff the watery stuff of *our acquaintance* is wet, whereas my doppelgänger's utterance of 'water is wet' is true iff the watery stuff of *their acquaintance* is wet. But our assumption is that a difference in truth-conditions is a difference in propositional content. So, supervenience fails, and my doppelgänger and I are in different wide mental states: I believe that the watery stuff of our acquaintance is wet, but my doppelgänger believes that the watery stuff of their acquaintance is wet.

3. Overcoming Incompatibilism

We are now in a position to see whether Boghossian is right that the semantic externalist is committed to the claim that natural kind concepts are object-dependent. The question is: do Dry Earthly tokens of sentences containing 'water' have truth-conditions? Suppose we settle for the combination of semantic externalism and referentialism. Then the answer is clearly negative. One can only pin down singular truth-conditions for sentences containing 'water' if 'water' is not empty: 'water is wet' is true iff ? is wet. What should occur on the right-hand side of the bi-conditional is the referent of 'water', but on Dry Earth tokens of 'water' fail to pick out anything. So, Boghossian is right that the semantic externalist must accept the claim that natural kind concepts are object-dependent, but only if she also accepts referentialism. If, on the other hand, she endorses causal descriptivism, then the answer to our question is positive. Just as one can give purely descriptive truth-conditions for Dry Earthly tokens of sentences containing 'water', one can give causally constrained, descriptive truth-conditions: 'water is wet' is true iff the watery stuff of their acquaintance is wet. On Dry Earth there is no watery stuff which the inhabitants interact with, but it is still true that had there been such a stuff, then it would have been the referent of their tokens of 'water'. So, if the semantic externalist accepts causal descriptivism, then she is not committed to the claim that natural kind concepts are object-dependent.

Where does this place us in relation to the MC-form? Suppose again that M is the state I am in when I think that water is wet, and that C is the proposition that water exists. Take first the strong form of semantic externalism according to which natural kind concepts are object-dependent. On this view, (2) is clearly a priori knowable. Both Twin Earth and Dry Earth are thought-experiments carried out from the armchair. This means that if one holds both this strong form of semantic externalism and Privileged Access, then one is hostage to instances of the MC-form. The proper response is clearly to give up on Privileged Access, i.e. to accept that (1) is merely a posteriori knowable. Which singular proposition I express by 'water is wet' is dependent upon which particular environment I am embedded in, and so I cannot know which singular proposition I express unless I not only sustain causal links with that environment, but also have appropriate empirical knowledge of it; cf. also McLaughlin & Tye (1998). Compare with indexical sentences. I cannot know a priori which singular proposition I express by 'you were here yesterday' since I have to know something about who the hearer is, what day it is, and where I am.

What I can know a priori is the linguistic meaning of the indexicals, e.g. that 'yesterday' always refers to the day before the day of the context of utterance. So, if the Semantic Externalist opts for Referentialism, then she should deny the a priority of (1).

Now take the weak form of semantic externalism according to which natural kind concepts are object-independent. On this view, (1) is clearly a priori knowable. To think that water is wet is to think that the watery stuff of our acquaintance is wet. But one can know this causally constrained, descriptive proposition a priori. All it takes is knowledge of which properties are associated with 'water' by competent speakers, where such competence involves *inter alia* knowledge of how to describe thought-experiments. Twin Earth tells us that if water exists, then water is the watery stuff of our acquaintance. But to know that is not to have empirical knowledge about one's particular environment; it is just to have the kind of knowledge that constitutes understanding the term. My doppelgänger on Twin Earth and I associate the same properties with 'water', and so I can know which properties are associated without knowing which particular environment I am embedded in. The fact that my doppelgänger expresses a different causally constrained, descriptive proposition by 'water is wet' does therefore not mean that I cannot know a priori which proposition I express by that sentence. All it means is that we are in different environments. But we have seen that (2) is false on this view. One can pin down causally constrained, descriptive truth-conditions even on Dry Earth, and so, one can believe that water is wet even if there is no water. So, if the semantic externalist opts for causal descriptivism, then she should deny the truth of (2).

The upshot is that once we get clear on the semantics of natural kind terms, we can either go for a strong form of semantic externalism in which case we must give up on Privileged Access, or we can stick to Privileged Access in which case we must rest content with a weak form of semantic externalism. The MC-form only poses a threat if we subscribe to both Privileged Access and the strong form of semantic externalism.[7]

Notes

1. I shall use '< >' brackets to indicate talk of concepts.
2. Burge (1979) made another two extensions of Putnam's Twin Earth argument (1975). First, his arthritis argument showed that content could be made dependent on facts in one's social environment, and secondly, that even the contents of non-natural kind terms are externally individuated. I will, however, restrict myself to the kind of Semantic Externalism that is underwritten by the Twin Earth argument.
3. I shall henceforth use 'a priori' to characterise the kind of knowledge involved in Privileged Access and so side-step the issue of whether 'non-empirical' is the more appropriate term. See Wright (1998) for more on Privileged Access.
4. Davies (1998) and Wright (2000) have argued that the warrant for (1) fails to transmit across the entailment in (2) to the conclusion in (3), because the MC-form in a sense begs the question against someone who claims that (1) and (2) are a priori knowable. What I shall argue is, however, that no one should claim that both (1) and (2) are a priori knowable in the first place.
5. The intuition that (3) is not a priori knowable is not universally shared. See e.g. Saywer (1998).
6. We assume that Twin Earth is a remote planet in the actual world. If Twin Earth is taken as a planet in a counterfactual world, then we need a rigidification device in order to ensure correct reference, e.g. the actual watery stuff. See also Jackson (1998).
7. Thanks to Lars Binderup, Lars Gundersen, Patrick Greenough, Duncan Pritchard, Sven Rosenkranz and Crispin Wright.

References

Boghossian, P. (1997) What the Externalist can Know A priori, *Proceedings of the Aristotelian Society*, pp. 161-175.
Burge, T. (1979) Individualism and the Mental, *Midwest Studies in Philosophy*, Vol. IV, pp. 73-122.
Burge, T. (1988) Individualism and Self-Knowledge, *The Journal of Philosophy*, 85, pp. 649-663.
Davidson, D. (1987) Knowing One's Own Mind, *Proceedings and Addresses of the American Philosophical Association*, 61, pp. 441-458.
Davies, M.: 'Externalism, Architectualism and Epistemic Warrant' in C. MacDonald, B. C. Smith & C. Wright (eds.) *Knowing our Own Minds*, pp. 321-361.
Jackson, F. (1998) References and Descriptions Revisited, *Philosophical Perspectives*, 12, *Language, Mind, and Ontology*, pp. 201-218.
Lewis, D. (1979) De Se Attitudes and De Dicto Attitudes, *Philosophical Review*, LXXXVIII, pp. 513-543.
C. MacDonald, B. C. Smith & C. Wright (eds.) (1998) *Knowing our Own Minds* (Oxford, Clarendon Press).
McKinsey, M. (1991) Anti-Individualism and Privileged Access, *Analysis* 51, pp. 9-16.
McLaughlin, B. & Tye, M.: Externalism, Twin-Earth and Self-Knowledge, in C. MacDonald, B. C. Smith & C. Wright (eds.) *Knowing Our Own Minds*, pp. 285-320.
Putnam, H. (1975) The 'Meaning of 'Meaning', in his *Philosophical Papers*, Vol. 2 (Cambridge, Cambridge University Press), pp. 215-271.
Sawyer, S. (1998) Privileged Access to the World, *Australasian Journal of Philosophy*, 76, pp. 523-33.
Wright, C. Self-Knowledge: The Wittgensteinian Legacy, in C. MacDonald, B. C. Smith & C. Wright (eds.) *Knowing Our Own Minds*, pp. 13-45.
Wright, C. (2000) Cogency and Question-Begging: Some Reflections on McKinsey's Paradox and Putnam's Proof, *Philosophical Issues*, 10.

QUASIREALISM OR MINIMALISM?[1]

LARS BINDERUP

University of Southern Denmark, Odense

An antirealist about ethics denies that there is a robust external grounding for ethical discourse. Our moral judgements have, in a sense, no external sanction. A central question for antirealism is whether it is possible to accept this lack of an external grounding while defending the hanging on to what Simon Blackburn has called *the propositional surface* of ethical discourse. That is, the fact that we practise in ethical discourse as if there is nothing inappropriate whatsoever in using notions like assertion, truth, belief, proposition and knowledge or in using standard deductive logic in an ethical context. The big challenge for an antirealist who wants to save this propositional surface is to account for the fact that the propositional surface is *common* to both discourses about which we want to be realists and discourses about which we want to be antirealists while not selling out to the realist by loosing sight of all the realism-relevant *differences*.

In this paper I shall discuss two antirealist strategies that share this ambition to save truth for ethics and hopefully go a little way towards assessing their relative merits. The main topic of discussion will be Blackburn's quasi-realist version of ethical expressivism where the strategy is to develop *a sorted notion of proposition* to capture the realism-relevant differences between discourses. I shall, however, in the later stages of the discussion draw on another formulation of cognitivist antirealism – the minimalism of Crispin Wright – where the central idea is to adopt *a sorted notion of truth* instead. The following discussion is, therefore, primarily a discussion internal to the antirealist camp – to which, I should add, I consider myself to belong.

1. Desiderata for an antirealist account of ethical discourse

Blackburn has likened choosing the best philosophical account of something to finding a way of getting all the pieces of a jigsaw puzzle 'to fit in a natural and satisfying way'. Let me, before I turn to the discussion of antirealism and truth, try to line up the most important pieces in the antirealist puzzle – partly in order to outline the background for what comes after and partly in the vain hope that antirealism about ethical discourse might come to seem at least *prima facie* attractive to readers who are still outside the antirealist camp.

The first important piece in the antirealist puzzle is the well-known set of arguments against *Moral Platonism* – i.e. non-reductive moral realism. That is, arguments purporting to exclude the possibility that ethical discourse is fit for representing robustly real, non-natural (*sui generis*) ethical facts. First of all, as Mackie has argued, the queerness of such facts should make us refuse to allow them into our ontology due to their being absolutely unlike anything we know from our ordinary and scientific dealings with the world – that is, they would have to belong to a mysterious supernatural Platonic part of reality hovering over and above nature with a peculiar ability to motivate us just by being known. And anyway, how can we account for the fact that we get to know about this supernatural reality without – implausibly – postulating the existence of a special intuitive moral faculty? Another problem for the Platonist is that he seems unable to explain a fact that is agreed on by all in the debate, namely that moral properties exhibit a kind of a priori supervenience on natural properties.[2] Ethical discourse, in short, cannot – contrary to what the Platonist believes – be grounded in something 'above' nature.

A second piece of the antirealist puzzle is that ethics cannot be grounded in nature either. The natural world, according to the antirealist, is thoroughly disenchanted – austerely physical and value-free, running its course without any consideration for human right or wrong. Any attempt to reduce the content of moral terms to the content of terms apt for *merely describing* (as opposed to evaluating) this natural world will miss out the evaluative content of moral judgements. The antirealist, thus, typically believes that Moore – with his open question argument – has shown us that *reductive forms of naturalism* simply will not succeed.[3] It should be added, though, that despite this rejection of reductive forms of naturalism it is also typically a central ambition of an antirealist to fit the account of ethics into a general *naturalistic account of reality*. The antirealist thus typically wants to describe and explain the phenomenon of moral discourse in naturalistic terms – as we shall see later – without reducing moral terms to naturalistic terms.

These first two pieces of the puzzle jointly entail that with respect to ethics it cannot be the case that 'truth is out there' in any substantial sense. True ethical statements cannot be representing *robust* facts for these facts could neither be natural facts nor supernatural facts and – as the antirealist would ask – what other kind of robust fact could there be for moral statements to represent?

Let me briefly mention two more pieces that the antirealist typically wants to fit into his puzzle. A satisfactory antirealist theory ought to take into account the *practical* nature of the moral language game. Thus, it is an important fact about the moral language game that it functions as a means to achieve practical coordination of life within communities. That is why the states we express in moral discourse must be seen by the antirealist account to be states that exert direct motivational pressure on action. But it is also a fact that moral discourse has a *propositional or truth-apt* surface. The linguistic transactions that are part of the moral language game appear to use propositions as their common currency. We as a matter of fact present our moral views as being true and we engage in reasoned debate with people who disagree with us. In the course of this debate we not only assert moral views, but we also consider moral hypotheses and deduce consequences from them – that is, we let moral sentences appear in unasserted contexts like that of the antecedents of conditionals. In addition, we apply truth-functional and other kinds of logic in moral reasoning and so on. So, a final important piece of the puzzle is that moral discourse at least *appears* to deal in propositional contents.

2. Blackburn's quasirealist version of expressivism on a thumbnail

An *expressivist* antirealist is someone who takes as his starting point the thesis that the states of mind expressed in moral discourse are practical states that contrast with cognitive states like beliefs. Now how might an *expressivist* antirealist of this kind fit the pieces of the antirealist jigsaw puzzle together? I shall not discuss in any great detail *the revisionist version* of expressivism that declares that the propositional surface of moral discourse is a fraud – that it is a *mere* surface hiding the real nature of what goes on in moral discourse – and proposes to revise actual moral practice accordingly. First of all, we ought not follow the revisionist in throwing away a piece of the puzzle – in this case the propositional character of moral discourse – unless we are compelled to do so. That is, we should always try to save as many of our original intuitions as possible while only discounting an intuition, if we can save more, or more important, *other* intuitions by doing so. Philosophers ought – in so far as possible – to leave things as they are, i.e. to include as many nice pieces of the puzzle as possible into the final picture. And Blackburn's *quasirealist version of expressivism,* as well as Wright's moral minimalism, attempt to show us how *all* the nice pieces *can* fit together – how it is possible to save the propositional surface in an antirealist setting – and before these projects have been proved irretrievably flawed, revisionism is not an interesting alternative.

Secondly, we may find this revisionist proposal wrongheaded for both prudential and moral reasons. For could we really allow – whether from a morally committed point of view or a prudential point of view – the throwing away of the propositional surface of moral discourse and thereby the possibility of reasoned debate about moral issues and the possibility of *peacefully* achieving a coordination of our practical lives? So let me turn to a short presentation of quasirealist expressivism.

According to Blackburn's expressivist,[4] we should view our moral sensibilities as *practical functional* states. They are functions taking as input a belief – a description of a natural state of affairs – and giving as output an attitude (or, to complete the picture, taking as input an attitude and giving as output an attitude). Attitudes are themselves motivational states and, therefore, they at least in normal circumstances exert direct pressure on action. Thus, they influence and govern our practical lives directly. Further, we voice our attitudes in public moral debate. We express our output attitudes by giving moral verdicts about particular actions, situations and characters and we express our background functional states – our basic moral sensibility – by avowing our moral standards and principles. Through voicing our moral sensibility and engaging in normative debate we can, at least sometimes, achieve the coordination of our attitudes with those of other people in our community and hence achieve a shared direction to our communal lives.

The expressivist story so far, hence, has already fitted in two pieces of the puzzle – certainly the practicality of moral discourse, but also we can glean how he can manage to fit morality into nature. For it is obviously possible to give a naturalistic account of our moral natures as they have just been described. In particular, it would seem that an explanation of *why* we have these moral natures could be given by evolutionary biology. Having a moral sensibility has been an evolutionary advantage in that it makes possible the achievement of a practical consensus that facilitates peaceful cooperation and therefore the reaping of the benefits of cooperation. Of course, a naturalistic explanation of this kind places morality in nature without presupposing the possibility of a naturalistic *reduction* of moral concepts.

Moral attitudes thus, according to the expressivist, play a very different role in our lives from the states of mind that we express in for example scientific and everyday discourse about our natural surroundings. When we believe things about for example atoms and apples, we aim at *literally representing* the facts. We try *literally to describe* facts that are out there independently of our human natures. Here talk of expressing beliefs is appropriate. By contrast, when we voice a moral attitude, it is not appropriate to speak – at least initially – of literal description nor, accordingly, to speak of the expression of beliefs. Moral attitudes and moral discourse are there to govern our lives with others, not to represent our natural surroundings. The assimilation of moral attitudes to beliefs would therefore show insensitivity to the actual role of the moral language game in our lives – an insensitivity of the kind that Wittgenstein warned philosophers against.

Having made this initial contrast between kinds of mental state – motivational moral *attitudes* versus genuinely representational *beliefs* – and correspondingly between descriptive and non-descriptive kinds of language game, the task of accounting for the common propositional surface of descriptive and non-descriptive discourse may have come to seem increasingly difficult. However, Blackburn's expressivist has got a plausible way of fitting in this last piece of the puzzle. He observes that the emergence of the ethical proposition is a result of the before mentioned need for moral public debate. The purpose of the ethical proposition is, in Blackburn's words, to 'act as a focus for practical thought'. When we debate we need to be able to do things like throw up moral hypotheses for discussion without asserting them. We need to avow conditional attitudes with unasserted antecedents. Generally, we need to be able to know the implications of our moral attitudes and therefore to be able to apply logical reasoning to our sets of moral attitudes and to make sense of the idea of consistency in a set of attitudes. And all these things are exactly what the ethical proposition can provide.

But how *can* the quasirealist get an ethical proposition from what is initially just a set of practical motivational attitudes? In particular, whereas it is straightforward to understand what goes on when we *assert* a moral sentence – that is we express a moral attitude and thereby commit ourselves in a certain way – it is more difficult to account for what happens when we use a moral sentence in an indirect or unasserted context. In the latter case we are exactly *not* expressing one of our attitudes or committing ourselves in any way. Does this not mean that the expressivist will have to tell a different story about moral sentences as they appear in asserted contexts as opposed to unasserted contexts?

Blackburn's solution is to point to the possibility of having more complex attitudes – namely the being in more complex, second-order, dispositional states towards combinations of attitudes. We 'tie ourselves to trees' as Blackburn expresses this by being in certain kinds of disjunctive dispositional states. If I, for instance, assent to a moral conditional 'If p then q' (where, say, p is a descriptive and q is a moral), I am according to this proposal in fact expressing my being tied to the tree of <either committing myself to q or accepting that *not-p*>. This amounts to giving expression to my being disposed to choose a given disjunct, whenever the other is closed off to me.

Examples of such dispositional states are the before mentioned functional states that make up our basic moral sensibility – the functional states taking us from a belief (or an attitude) to an attitude. We express these states by avowing our moral standards. We say for instance that 'If killing is wrong then letting people die is wrong'. This is according to the quasirealist exactly the avowing of the complex dispositional state of being tied to the tree of <either committing oneself to the wrongness of letting people die or committing oneself to its not being wrong to kill>. This proposal also explains what it is to *disagree* about moral standards. Someone with a deontologically inspired moral sensibility might for instance refuse to be tied to the tree expressed by the standard 'If killing is wrong then letting people die is wrong' and in stead avow complex dispositions that reflect a moral distinction between killing and letting die.

Of course this notion of being tied to a tree corresponds nicely to the notion of accepting an ordinary disjunction where one is also tied to a similar semantic tree. So what the notion of being tied to a tree does is to help the quasirealist explain why we as a matter of fact use standard disjunctions and conditionals to express our moral functional states and why we apply the standard deductive procedures to such expressions. The central idea is that the standard logical structuring of sets of propositions mirrors the functional structure of our attitudes. Or at least near enough. To quote Blackburn: '… it is unnecessary to claim that we make no jump at all … All we have is sufficient similarity of logical role to make the temptation to exploit *ordinary* propositional logic quite irresistible – and that is what we do'.[5] Thus the quasirealist can, seemingly, starting from talk about attitudes give a plausible explanation of why the propositional surface of moral discourse has evolved. It is as if at some point in the development of human discourse we have found it useful to *borrow* the tool of propositional logic from other realistic, genuinely representational, discourses in order to keep track of our sets of moral attitudes and in order to engage in moral debate. Though the tool originally evolved because it helped us to keep track of our sets of robust beliefs about nature, it happened to be quite handy as a way of giving public expression to the sets of functionally ordered practical states that make up our ethical sensibility.

Having in this way saved the propositional surface of ethical discourse – in particular having made sense of the idea of logical inference and consistency in a set of attitudes – the quasirealist can now go on to make sense of the idea of *improvement* of one's moral sensibility. For Blackburn improvement is not only a question of getting rid of the inconsistencies in one's moral sensibility, though that of course is an important way of improving one's set of attitudes. We may, according to him, admire and rank a moral sensibility because of many other features – its sensitivity, flexibility, state of development or sophistication, coherency, liveability and so on. So there are many ways to achieve a better moral sensibility when we encounter other moral sensibilities and admire them to the extent that they inspire us into changing our own. Then, on the back of this idea of improvement of moral sensibilities, the quasirealist can finally define a constructive notion of *moral truth*. One suggestion has been that a commitment expressing an attitude U is true exactly when U belongs to *the best possible set of attitudes*. And the best possible set of attitudes is, of course, the set of attitudes that comes about when all possibilities of improvement have been exploited maximally.

One potential worry here is that this quasirealist account of improvement and truth entails a form of relativism, since talk of improvement will of course always be relative to a committed moral view – a given moral sensibility. But this is a misunderstanding. The very application of a truth predicate in the discourse compels us to 'argue and practise as though the truth is single',[6] and thus we are always entitled to express our moral disagreements with others directly, even when faced with radically different but seemingly consistent moral sensibilities. Also in this respect the quasirealist account appears to save the surface of the actual moral language game. Of course, nothing strictly speaking compels us to aim for ethical consistency and truth. The commitment to engage in truth-governed moral debate with other people – to try to improve our moral sensibilities and achieve practical coordination with them – is itself a first order moral commitment. The value of moral truth on this picture is, I take it, an instrumental value – a means to achieving a better moral sensibility where the notion of 'better' betrays that one is here already committed to a particular moral point of view.

The final part of the quasirealist story draws some of the consequences of having earned the right to a notion of truth in ethics. As Ramsey pointed out, once we have the ethical proposition and thus the ability to make moral assertions that *p*, we add no extra content by asserting that 'p' is true. And it is a mere paraphrase to climb even further up what Blackburn has called Ramsey's Ladder[7] and talk of *p* as 'corresponding to the facts' or 'literally describing things as they are' or the like. Likewise we trivially get the license to talk of belief and even knowledge, once we have earned the ethical proposition. But for Blackburn it is important to notice that although the quasirealist grants that since we have truth in ethics, we are licensed to climb up and down Ramsey's Ladder as much as we like when making ethical claims, he has not conceded anything to *the realist*. For we can agree with the deflationist that Ramsey's Ladder is lying horizontally on the ground, since the license to move up and down the steps is a result of mere linguistic convention.

Further, the quasirealist's acceptance of truth and all its paraphrases in ethics is not to be confused with the *quietist* refusal to draw any realism-relevant distinctions between the various discourses with a propositional surface – i.e. the quietist deconstruction of the realism-antirealism debate associated with deflationism about truth. The reason is that since the quasirealist gives *different accounts of the emergence of the proposition* in discourses about which realism is in order and in expressive discourses, he remains sensitive to the realism-relevant differences between discourses. What saves quasirealism from quietism is thus the adoption of a *sorted notion of proposition*. This strategy Blackburn in one place calls the Ramsey Option.[8]

3. Problems for quasirealist expressivism?

Having given this thumbnail sketch of how quasirealist expressivism proposes to fit the pieces of the antirealist puzzle together, I shall now turn to a discussion of the merits of quasirealism. There has been much controversy over the years about whether the quasirealist *can* successfully save the propositional surface of the moral language game. The discussion has become highly technical and I shall not attempt to enter into it in any great detail here. However, let me try to sum up the main dialectic by looking briefly at the quasirealist construal of a moral conditional. I shall be drawing on writings of Crispin Wright and Bob Hale as well as Blackburn in the following.[9]

There are two main ways for the expressivist to construe a moral conditional. A) He may analyse it in such a way that an attitude operator becomes the dominant operator (for instance H!(p→H!q), where H! is the 'hooray-operator' standing for approval). Or, alternatively, B) he may make the conditional operator into the operator with the largest scope. In the first case we say that what we avow when we avow a moral standard is really an attitude of approval towards a certain combination of attitudes – a higher order attitude. The problem on this account is that it is difficult to see that someone who, for instance, endorses *p* and endorses *if p then q* (where either *p* or *q* or both are moral sentences), yet fails to endorse *q*, is making a *logical* error. For what he is doing is merely failing to live up to his own higher order attitudes and that is at most a *moral and not a logical* failing. This inability of the construal to capture the logical failure is problematic, since it is certainly part of the propositional surface of moral discourse that people who fail to perform a moral modus ponens are *logically* inept and not just morally depraved. This, I believe was the problem with Blackburn's early theory in his *Spreading the Word*.

However, in the later work of Blackburn, the second possible construal of the moral conditional – with a dominant conditional operator – has been advanced. This is the idea already mentioned of construing moral conditionals as expressing the complex disjunctive states of being tied to a tree. Now, here there appears to be no problem of saving the ordinary conditional and disjunction and thus of finding *logical and not moral* error. But, on the other hand, it is not clear that, by doing so, the quasirealist avoids conceding to the minimalist that the operators found in moral discourse are really just standard truth-conditional operators and, correspondingly, that the notion of truth operative within the discourse is just our standard notion of truth rather than quasi-truth. It would seem that the 'quasi-bit' of the account stands in danger of being lost. But, for the purposes of the argument to follow, let me grant that the quasirealist *can* save the propositional surface of moral discourse by choosing this second strategy while remaining a *quasi*realist, though I shall return briefly to this point in the conclusion.

What I want to focus on is rather what happens once it is granted that the quasirealist succeeds in saving this surface. The interesting worry – recognised and explicitly addressed by Blackburn[10] – is that the whole quasirealist enterprise *bites its own tail*. It starts out by relying on a fundamental contrast between beliefs and attitudes. But after the propositional surface has been saved on the basis of this contrast, it seems that an attitude actually has become a kind of belief – at least attitudes now behave like beliefs in all the relevant ways. Or to use terms proposed by Blackburn himself: Having earned the moral proposition for us, the quasirealist now allows us to move from a *contrastive* notion of belief to an *inclusive* notion of belief – according to which attitudes (i.e. moral commitments) are a special form of belief.

I am not sure that this version of the tail-biting objection is the right way to locate the main problem for quasirealism (if there is such a problem). Even though the quasirealist wins through to the notions of moral belief, truth, proposition and so on, it is clear that he still has the means to draw contrasts between genuine propositions and constructed propositions. The seemingly heavy and realist-sounding notions of truth, fact and belief that he has earned for moral discourse were after all just the result of the linguistic conventions of Ramsey's Ladder. As already argued, this is not to concede anything to the realist.

So let me therefore attempt to locate a problem for the quasirealist in a slightly different place. The tail biting works, I want to suggest, in a different way to cause a problem for the quasirealist. The problem may be one of a (perhaps deliberate) scientistic bias in the quasirealist notion of a proposition. Part of the starting point for the quasirealist is the presupposition that the propositional surface in discourses apt for realistic interpretation – like scientific discourse – is completely unproblematic whereas it is a mystery that moral discourse has such a surface. This presupposition derives, it seems, from an underlying thesis that propositional surface is essentially and properly tied to literal description or genuine representation of the kind we presumably find in scientific discourse. *That* is why truth and propositional content has to be *earned* in moral discourse whereas we get it for free in scientific discourse. But then there *is* a kind of tail biting going on once the quasirealist project is carried out. Because the very fact that the quasirealist is able to save the propositional surface of a not genuinely representational discourse like moral discourse seems to show that propositional surface is *not* necessarily tied to representation and literal description – contrary to what was presupposed.

Perhaps another way to see that there is a bias in the quasirealist's initial assumptions is to consider this: On the quasirealist account it is as if before the quasirealist came along and *earned* the propositional surface of moral discourse, ordinary people applying logical inferences and the like when discussing moral issues were somehow *stealing* the propositional clothing rightly belonging to more seriously representational discourses. As if – in a very un-

Wittgensteinian way – the scientific, literally descriptive, language game can take care of itself whereas the moral language game – in particular its propositional surface – has to be propped up by philosophy.

4. A sorted notion of truth? – Wright's minimalism

What this objection may suggest is that a moral antirealist who wants to save the propositional surface of moral discourse ought to look for an account of proposition – and therefore trivially of truth-aptitude – that is not at the outset imbued with any realistic bias. Crispin Wright's non-deflationist minimalism about truthaptness and truth is an account that does just this.[11] What I want to do in the final part of this paper is to introduce and discuss this position as an alternative version of antirealism with truth. Whether we ought to choose minimalism over quasirealism will in the end be a question of which position is able to fit all the important pieces together in the most 'natural and satisfying way' – a way that solves most or all problems and avoids things like accusations of bias and scientism. I shall try to argue that minimalism is hard competition for the quasirealist by attempting to answer two objections on behalf of the minimalist.

Crucially, the minimalist does not accept that taking the propositional surface of a discourse at face value concedes anything whatsoever to the realist – not even seemingly. There is no realist bias in the notion of a proposition and thus there is no distinction between a discourse's *appearing* to be dealing in propositional contents and a discourse's *genuinely* dealing in propositional contents. Thus the minimalist sets up *two minimal conditions for being truth-apt* (or, equivalently, being assertoric or dealing in propositional contents). The first condition is that the discourse must display propositional surface *syntax* – that is, it must have all the syntactic features that enable its sentences to sustain standard truth-preserving inferential practices. The second requirement is that the discourse is governed by publicly acknowledged standards of warranted assertibility – that the discourse is *disciplined*, as Wright calls it. If there were no general consensus about what conditions justify the use of the sentences within a discourse – if there were no established public patterns of use of the sentences – there would simply be no reason to hold that the sentences have fixed contents at all, let alone truth-apt contents.

Of course, if the minimalist said no more at this point, he would end up as a quietist like the deflationist about truth. He would have no means of pointing to realism-relevant differences between discourses, since the adoption of such a 'promiscuous' notion of genuine truth-aptness or propositional content, in fact, amounts to giving up the possibility that we may draw realism-relevant distinctions at the level of the proposition – it amounts to giving up Blackburn's Ramsey Option. Wright's minimalist, however, is not a quietist and instead proposes to work with a *sorted notion of truth*.

The central claim about *truth* is here that all it takes to be a concept of truth is to satisfy the *platitudes* surrounding the concept. Platitudes are basic a priori and necessary truths involving the concept that any competent user of the concept must – at least on reflection – recognize. A short list of the platitudes surrounding the concept of truth could be as follows: Truth is *transparent* – that is, to assert is to present as true. Truth is *timeless* – if a proposition is true at one point in time, then it is always true and always was true. Truth is *absolute* in that it does not come in degrees. Truth-aptitude is *preserved under embedding*. If a sentence is truth-apt, then so is it when it is embedded in a negation, disjunction, conjunction, etc. Truth *differs from justification* – a claim can be justified but false and true but not justified. And finally, to be true is – in a trivial, non-substantial sense – to *correspond* to reality, to say things as they are, to fit the facts etc.

But how *can* truth on this account become sorted? The key idea is that, on the one hand, since all truth-predicates must satisfy the platitudes, truth is the *same* across different domains. But, on the other hand, minimalism makes possible a form of *pluralism about truth*. Not in the sense that the word 'truth' becomes ambiguous, but rather in the sense that we can have different – though formally uniform – concepts of truth operating in different areas of discourse. That is, different predicates can satisfy the platitudes when we consider different domains of discourse – and the property of truth can as a consequence be differently *constituted or realised* in different domains. Thus, for example, the property of truth in ethics and the property of truth in physics – though formally uniform – may be differently constituted.

And this is what allows the minimalist to fend off the quietist. It becomes possible to compare the claims to realism made on behalf of different discourses by focusing on the different truth-concepts and truth-realisers in the discourses and by asking how they differ with respect to *further* realism-relevant properties. Thus reshaped, realism-debates will revolve around the question whether the discourse can sustain a more *robust* truth-predicate of some kind – expressing a concept that captures various further realist intuitions.

Wright proposes that the realism-relevant features of the truth-predicates may be found by discussing questions like whether the truth-predicate is evidentially constrained or not, whether truth might be seen as constituted by the opinions of the best judges or not, whether it is *a priori* that at least one participant in a dispute formulated within the discourse has a cognitive shortcoming or not, or whether the facts represented in the discourse can explain other facts unmediated by agents with propositional attitudes or not. And if the realist wins such a discussion about a particular discourse, we can speak of more *robust* notions of truth (and of fact, representation and so on) being operative within the discourse.

Someone who accepts Wright's minimalist framework for realism debates as outlined here and has antirealist intuitions about moral discourse will then claim about moral discourse that whereas the discourse is assertoric and truth-apt in virtue of its propositional surface and its discipline, the truth-predicate operative within moral discourse is *merely minimal* – i.e. it is a kind of truth-predicate that does not capture any further realist intuitions. Wright's proposal is, thus, that an antirealist truth-predicate – more precisely that of 'superassertibility' – can satisfy the platitudes with respect to moral discourse. And just as the minimal notion of truth-aptitude carried no bias towards realism, this merely minimal notion of moral truth carries no realist content.

5. Defending minimalism against two objections

That completes the rough sketch of minimalism about ethics. In order to move towards a tentative conclusion on the question whether this offers serious competition to the quasirealist conception, let me attempt to indicate briefly how one might answer two objections against the minimalist proposal that have been advanced in the literature and referred to with approval by Blackburn.[12]

The first – due to Christine Tappolet[13] – asks whether the minimalist's pluralism about truth does not have a problem with accounting for the validity of arguments where the premises come from different discourses with different truth-predicates. The answer to this must be that since both the truth-predicates in play in such an argument satisfy the platitudes they are both genuine truth-predicates and what is transferred from the premises to the conclusion in a valid argument is simply *truth*. It is a mistake to think that somehow the fact that the truth-property may be differently constituted in different discourses makes the word 'truth' ambiguous. Wright uses a helpful analogy with the concept of identity to make this point clear.[14] What constitutes identity between numbers and what constitutes identity between persons, for example, are clearly very different things. But this does not in any way suggest that identity is an ambiguous notion as it is applied to different kinds of objects. In fact – the suggestion is – the concept of identity has the kind of formal unity while being multiply realisable that the minimalist suggests truth has. All uses of the concept of identity must comply with certain platitudes – the logical laws of the indiscernibility of identicals and of universal reflexivity – in the same way as any truth-predicate must comply with the platitudes mentioned above. So, I suggest, the minimalist can trivially meet the first objection.

The second objection – due to Michael Smith, Frank Jackson and Graham Oppy (*the Australians* in the following)[15] and answered by both Wright and Divers and Miller[16] – tries to cause problems for the minimalist by showing that he, even by his own standards, muscles out the expressivist from his framework for the realism-debates too soon. The objection exploits the fact that the minimalist is platitudinously committed to a notion of moral belief via accepting the truth-aptness of moral discourse. This is because of the true principle (P):

> (P) If s is truth-apt, then s can be used to express the content of a belief

In other words, due to the platitudes the minimalist is compelled to use *an inclusive notion of belief*.

The crucial move in the Australian objection is to use contraposition on the conditional (P). In particular, they point out that it is possible for the expressivist to argue that, since the states expressed by moral sentences *cannot be beliefs* due to their internal connection with motivation and action – this we have learned from Hume – ethical sentences cannot be truth-apt despite the fact that they are disciplined and have the appropriate syntax. So discipline and propositional surface does not suffice for genuine truth-aptitude and the expressivist is back in the picture. The argument can be summarised thus:

(1) The states expressed by the sincere utterance of moral sentences are intrinsically motivational.
(2) No belief is intrinsically motivational.

∴ The states expressed by the sincere utterance of moral sentences are not beliefs.

∴ Moral sentences are not truth-apt (via contraposition on (P))

If the minimalist now tries to defend his expressivist-unfriendly framework for the realism-debates by denying that Hume was right when he said that beliefs could not be motivational it would become clear – the objection continues – that there is a cognitivist bias in the shape of a substantial anti-Humean theory of moral psychology built into the minimalist's framework. The minimalist in that case has been stacking the cards against the expressivist by assuming an anti-Humean moral psychology.

Now to answer this objection, I think it is important to see that whereas the minimalist is certainly compelled to use an inclusive notion of belief, he also has the means to make distinctions between *kinds* of belief parallel to the distinctions between degrees of robustness of truth-predicates. We can thus define a general inclusive notion of *minimal belief* as what is expressed by sentences formulated within any truth-apt discourse. But, we can also define *robust beliefs* as belonging to the subclass of minimal beliefs that are expressed in discourses apt for more robust notions of truth. Thus, we may have a contrast within the inclusive notion of minimal belief between robust beliefs (perhaps with varying degrees of robustness) and merely minimal beliefs.

Then we must ask: Does the objection go through once we distinguish between merely minimal belief and robust belief? Consider that the following principle is a platitude:

(P*) If s is truth-apt, then s can be used to express the content of a minimal belief

But, notice then that the second premise of the argument of the Australian objection becomes false, if we interpret 'belief' uniformly as minimal belief. That is, it is simply not true that:

(2*) No *minimal* belief is intrinsically motivational

since some minimal beliefs are moral beliefs and they are arguably intrinsically motivational. So, if we consistently interpret 'belief' in the objection as *minimal* belief, the argument will not go through.

On the other hand, we can make the second premise true by using here the notion of a robust belief and claiming truly that

(2**) No *robust* belief is intrinsically motivational.

(By the way, perhaps that was the real point of the Humean theory). But, then there is a problem with the appropriately modified version of (P). That is,

(P**) If s is truth-apt, then s can be used to express the content of a robust belief

is clearly not a platitude, since *s* might be truth-apt while only being apt for expressing merely minimal beliefs. A discourse's being minimally truth-apt is simply not sufficient for it's being apt to express robust beliefs. So it would seem that the minimalist could answer this second – Australian – objection by developing a distinction between merely minimal and robust beliefs – since the argument will not go through with a consistent interpretation of the term 'belief' as this term figures in the original objection.

As already mentioned, in the end the dispute between the minimalist and the quasirealist must be decided by weighing the weaknesses and the strengths of the two ways of formulating antirealism with truth against each other. There is no hope that an easy knockdown argument will settle the dispute. All I can claim to have done here is to have shown that minimalism is still in the running since it *can* answer two recent objections. Antirealists about ethics wanting to save truth in ethical discourse therefore, for all that has been said in the foregoing, still face a choice between endorsing quasirealism or endorsing (non-deflationist) minimalism. What might ultimately tip the scale in favour of one or the other version of moral antirealism? It would appear that a lot – if not everything – turns on the issue, shelved in section 3, of whether the expressivist can give a quasirealist account of moral conditionals that meets all the objections while avoiding to concede to the minimalist that the notions of truth and logical inference operative within moral discourse are, after all, *genuine* notions of truth and logical inference and not merely *quasi*-notions.

Notes

1. This paper is a slightly revised version of the paper given at the Annual Meeting of the Danish Philosophical Association at Roskilde University, February 2002. I wish to thank the participants in the ensuing discussion.
2. Blackburn 1984, 182-87, and 1985. I discuss and attempt to improve on the supervenience argument against non-naturalist moral realism in Binderup 2003.
3. This leaves, of course, *non-reductive* forms of naturalism – Cornell style naturalism – that are not touched by Moore's argument. However, there are independent problems for this type of naturalism, see e.g. Blackburn 1985 and 1998 and Binderup 2000 and 2003.
4. For a general presentation of Blackburn's quasirealist version of expressivism, see Blackburn 1984 and 1998.

5. Blackburn 1988, 197, his italics.
6. Blackburn 1984, 201.
7. E.g. Blackburn 1998, 294-98.
8. See Blackburn 1998.
9. See Hale 1986, 1993, Wright 1995 and Blackburn 1988, 1993b.
10. E.g. Blackburn 1993b, 366.
11. Wright 1993, 1995, 1998.
12. Blackburn 1997, 160, 167.
13. Tappolet 1997.
14. Wright 1995, 6-8.
15. Jackson, Oppy and Smith 1994.
16. Divers and Miller 1994 and 1995, and Wright 1998.

References

Binderup, Lars. 2000. *Moral Minimalism*. Ph.D. thesis. (Unpublished).
Binderup, Lars. 2003. Supervenience, Reduction and the Case for Moral Realism. (Unpublished).
Blackburn, Simon. 1984. *Spreading the Word*. Oxford: Oxford University Press.
Blackburn, Simon. 1985. Supervenience Revisited. In Blackburn 1993a.
Blackburn, Simon. 1988. Attitudes and Content. In Blackburn 1993a.
Blackburn, Simon. 1993a. *Essays in Quasi-Realism*. Oxford: Oxford University Press.
Blackburn, Simon. 1993b. Realism, Quasi or Queasey? in Haldane and Wright 1993.
Blackburn, Simon. 1997. Wittgenstein, Wright, Rorty and Minimalism. *Mind*, vol. 107.
Blackburn, Simon. 1998. *Ruling Passions*. Oxford: Oxford University Press.
Divers, John and Miller, Alexander. 1994. Why Expressivists about Value Should Not Love Minimalism about Truth. *Analysis*, vol. 54.1, 12-19.
Divers, John and Miller, Alexander. 1995. Platitudes and Attitudes. *Analysis*, vol. 55.1, 37-44.
Haldane, John and Wright, Crispin (eds.). 1993. *Reality, Representation and Projection*. Oxford: Oxford University Press.
Hale, Bob. 1986. The Compleat Projectivist. *Philosophical Quarterly*, vol. 36.142, 65-84.
Hale, Bob. 1993. Can There Be a Logic of Attitudes? in Haldane and Wright 1993.
Jackson, F., Oppy, G. and Smith, M. 1994. Minimalism and Truthaptness. *Mind*, vol. 103, 287-302.
Tappolet, Christine. 1997. Mixed Inferences: a Problem for Pluralism About Truth Predicates. *Analysis* 57.3, 209-10.
Wright, Crispin. 1992. *Truth and Objectivity*. Cambridge, Mass.: Harvard University Press.
Wright, Crispin. 1995. Truth in Ethics. *Ratio* (New Series), vol.8, December 1995, 209-26.
Wright, Crispin. 1998. Comrades against Quietism. *Mind*, vol. 107, 183-203.

THE ETHICS OF UNDERSTANDING

NIELS THOMASSEN

Department of Philosophy and the Studies of Religion
University of Southern Denmark
e-mail: nith@filos.sdu.dk

Preliminaries

The good consists of doing good and omitting to do evil. The evil consists of doing evil or omitting to do good. To do good means contributing to the furthering of happiness, well-being, or love of life. Or, to put it briefly, contributing to furthering happiness in the world and combatting unhappiness. Furthering happiness is not primarily achieved by helping others to experience certain things, as utilitarians would generally claim, but by involving them in activities by means of which their lives succeed. Correspondingly, one furthers one's own happiness by seeking those activities, forms of work, interpersonal communication and challenges by means of which one's own life succeeds.

Responsibility is something one has as far as one has power or influence. In immediate interpersonal communication each of us has power. This is because all such interaction takes place within various relations of dependency or power. Minimum dependency results from all communication with others containing an element of self-surrender. Surrendering oneself means making oneself dependent; accepting appeals from others means assuming influence. This fact is the cornerstone of the ethics of the Danish philosopher K.E. Løgstrup[1]. Although there are other forms of power generally found in interpersonal communication, which is neglected by Løgstrup. A considerable number of our actions take place within some of the hierarchical structures that permeate our society, i.e. within power relations that are given in advance. Let us call them suprapersonal power relations (Habermas calls them supremacy relations). Added to which there is the power of the human personality and the influence and power relations that a shared history establishes – what might be called the 'pecking order' of the relationship.

The action which is ethically correct handles the power and dependency relations of communication in such a way that the happiness of those involved is taken into account equally. This is a demand for what could be called ethical solidarity. Norms can be seen as summing up the experiences of the race, but the crucial thing is not, as deontologists generally claim, complying with certain obligations. It is, on the contrary, making an active effort on behalf of those people, including oneself, who are involved in the interpersonal communication. If one is to choose between acting in one context or another, taking care of one's family or of the outcasts of society, then one has to try to assess where one's efforts will have the greatest value[2].

In this sense the good consists in doing good, the evil in doing evil. But a prerequisite for being able to do good or evil to others is that one understands what it is that does them good or evil. One has to be capable of sympathetic insight into and of sharing their joys and sorrows. In this sense understanding is a prerequisite for all ethics. This also applies to oneself, insofar as one is talking of obligations or responsibility for oneself. To which could be added that one can only be responsible for what one does to the extent that one is able to understand oneself.

That which I am summing up here by the term 'understanding' means being able to understand in the narrow sense of the word, i.e. using the intellect to see something clearly, but also the ability to identify oneself with and share the joys and sorrows of others. The capacity for empathy is another way of putting it. And both aspects involve the imagination, by the way. So one could talk of humanity in a broad sense. In the following I will also continue to use the word understanding as a composite term.

An understanding humanity of this kind is a necessary substratum for all ethics. A brief indication of this: The fundamental demand of the utilitarians has to do with results in the form of promoting pleasure, satisfying preferences, or the like. Although utilitarianism – perhaps on the basis of scientific prejudices – often neglects the fact, the preferences and satisfaction of others are not matters of course, but are given as a task for sympathetic understanding. In Kant's ethics the problem is the same, although reversed. Obligation is defined as being the opposite of inclinations. The struggle against inclinations presupposes an understanding of them. Insofar as Kant sees it as an obligation to take care of other people's well-being, understanding is also part of a more positive context. Even for the ethical egoist the happiness and unhappiness of others plays a role, since one cannot further one's own interests independently of others, or, to formulate it more brutally, one cannot use the happiness or unhappiness of others in one's own plans without a certain understanding of them. I do not intend to pursue this idea further here.

The following will concentrate instead on a general investigation of the importance of understanding for ethics.

First and foremost, understanding and its use are not just a matter of course. Understanding others often means making an effort. There is a wide range from the simple to the complicated. Apart from the considerable individual differences in how well one is equipped in this respect, an understanding of other people's interests, passions and opinions, their secret hopes and anxieties, does not necessarily come by itself. In that respect there is a need to make demands of the understanding.

So one could say that ethics falls into two halves. The first demand of all ethics is that one must understand the happiness and unhappiness of the parties involved. After which there are the truly ethical demands, formulated earlier in the basic demand for ethical solidarity. Let me call the former the ethics of understanding, the latter true or proper ethics, or simply the first and second layers of ethics. My main interest here is in the former.

What is understanding?

There is a necessary relationship between understanding and meaning[3]. Understanding is always understanding of meaning. Meaning is a phenomenon in its intelligibility. Meaning is an entity *sui generis*. Using Løgstrup's word for linguistic meaning one could characterize it as a view, i.e. an orientation, but that does not say all that much[4]. Meaning does not have an independent existence. It is not an ontological category. But nor is meaning something that is added, attached to phenomena. In an action one can differentiate between behaviour and meaning, but not separate them. Action is not anything without its meaning. The movements, the behaviour, that may possibly be left if one excludes meaning are not themselves action. On the contrary, an action is a meaning manifested in behaviour. The idealism that reduces the action to spiritual meaning and the materialism, e.g. behaviourism, that reduces it to behaviour are both making a mistake. Meaning cannot be reduced to intention, since matter, situation and communicative context add to the meaning of an action. The meaning of an action can also, by the way, have many aspects of, for example, a matter-of-fact[5], esthetic, political and religious nature. – Here I choose to ignore the type of meaning that exists in pure concepts, thought content, scientific laws, mathematical entities, etc.

Understanding can be directed to many other things besides persons. Human communication takes place not least as a result of a whole series of matter-of-fact contexts. Teaching, for example, is not only personal communication; it is communication about a matter-of-fact content: physics, creative art, philosophy, or whatever. Corresponding matter-of-fact mediation takes place in practically all forms of human communication. H.-G. Gadamer sees understanding as being solely a matter-of-fact sharing, i.e. sharing of a matter. For him understanding always has a matter as its subject, while an understanding of man at best can only be an auxiliary discipline when matter-of-fact understanding fails[6]. But understanding persons is of importance in matter-of-fact mediated communication as well. This was realized by the reconstruction hermeneutics of the 19th century, which dealt with sympathetic insight into and reconstruction of mental or spiritual content in phenomena. Gadamer's revolt against this view is linked to its positivist strain, that it does not have any sense of subjectivity's, i.e. pre-understanding's, productive importance in understanding. This draws a veil over the fact that the hermeneutics of the 19th century had a different interest than Gadamer's matter hermeneutics, namely to understand human life, whether it was thought of as mental life or the unfolding of the human spirit. A closer look at the relationship between the understanding of persons and matters cannot avoid taking the form of a partial rehabilitation of "reconstruction hermeneutics".

One can find examples of communication without matter-of-fact mediation in unfounded aggression and unreserved eroticism. This does not, however, mean that they are devoid of understanding.

Understanding can also apply to situations and actions, art, religion, language, history, etc. I intend, however, to restrict myself mainly to understanding of persons, even though other aspects of understanding are relevant to ethics.

Understanding in its broad sense has, as mentioned, three components, i.e. sympathetic insight, imagination and understanding in the narrow sense. Understanding in the narrow sense has two elements, which could be called comprehension and acquisition. To take an example: my beloved has been raped and relates the incident in utter despair. One thing that happens is that I feel and suffer along with her pain; I identify myself sympathetically and understandingly with it. Another thing that happens is that I react, am filled with compassion and anger, resulting in action: taking care of her, thinking about whether to report the incident, what ought to be done with the perpetrator, etc. I understand the violation as something that has importance for me, makes demands of me, involves me. This makes me also understand myself as the one of whom demands are being made and one who can do something. I call this acquisition, since it is first and foremost this which Kierkegaard has in mind when he says that truth is subjectivity or acquisition[7].

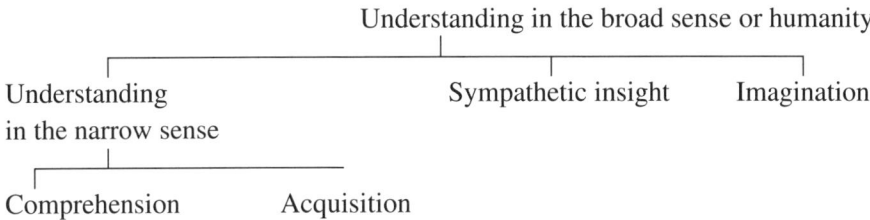

Comprehension is identifying, without self-understanding and receptive, whereas acquisition is distancing, contains self-understanding and is productive. The receptivity of comprehension consists in its submitting to that which is comprehended. In terms of action it is inactive or passive. The productivity of acquisition consists in its suggesting alternatives. In terms of action it is active and creative.

Comprehension is in all understanding. Acquisition, on the other hand, may be lacking, as is the case in identifying relations with models, idols, etc. But full understanding contains both elements. Comprehension is directed towards and deals with the reality of the other person. In that sense it is objective and helps to ensure objectivity in acquisition as well. Existential philosophy overlooks comprehension and thereby has problems with objectivity in understanding. This also applies to Gadamer.

Sympathetic insight has the nature of an emotive identification with the person. It consists as it were of allowing oneself to be tuned by the emotive state of the other person. It presupposes an openness in the understanding person, an access to the tuned soundboard of the mind. This same openness can of course be misused by the other person. Or, in other words, it is intimately linked with the vulnerability of the individual.

Sympathetic insight is closely related to comprehension, even blending with it in many contexts. Despite this fact, I feel that they should be kept separate. Understanding of a matter includes comprehension, but not sympathetic insight, which is linked to the understanding of human beings. Communication can take place without sympathetic insight, however. Teaching, trade, administration often stick to the level of understanding. Normal conversation does not assume sympathetic insight either. Understanding is activated by every form of meaning; sympathetic insight by the emotive state of the other person.

Sympathetic insight does not consist in comprehending the other person's joys or sorrows, but of partaking in them. In a way it is not as receptive and passive as comprehension. On the other hand it is not really distancing. It does not include self-understanding and is not productive or creative as regards action.

The imagination can, with Kierkegaard in mind, be characterized as the medium of the infinite-making, i.e. it is the ability to disregard that which is given[8]. This can take place in many different forms, as can be seen, for example, from a study of artistic styles and genres, and in many respects, such as the throwing up of alternatives, fantasizing, or humour.

In practice, sympathetic insight, imagination and understanding are all intricately interwoven, with pure forms only occurring in marginal cases. Emotive identification with a person, for example, nearly always involves understanding. One is not only moved by the joy or sorrow of the other person; one also understands what one is moved by and with. Conversely, both comprehension and acquisition in the understanding of human beings often contains elements of sympathetic insight. The three types of relations should rather be characterized as aspects of one and the same extensive relationship: understanding in the broad sense. Retaining this terminology is not arbitrary.

The interaction of understanding and ethics

The two layers of ethics work together, but the relationship between them can be pretty complicated for all that. As already mentioned, ethical responsibility is determined by understanding. Yet differences crop up already here. For certain ethical demands can be met with a minimum of understanding. One can refrain from killing for the simple reason that one knows that it is a punishable offence. One can speak the truth simply because it is one's nature to do so, or because one has been indoctrinated to do so. In such instances the right thing is done without any understanding of those affected by the action. Conversely, one cannot advise a friend about marital problems without understanding him, his wife and children, as well as their general situation. Nor can one bring children up to be free and independent persons or advise young people about a choice of education without understanding. In such situations general ethical norms and values can at the most only be a guide.

If one looks at literature and films, a considerable part of their interest is precisely in complicated events, where clear ethical rules fall short, where the question of guilt is virtually impossible to settle, or where there simply is nothing to refer to except one's own personal humanity. All of these are scenarios where understanding is vital for both parties involved, the agents and the audience.

Part of our need to be able to find our directions in the world is bound up with being able to distinguish between good and evil. We have to know where to place our sympathy, who we are to help, where we are to make our effort in a given conflict. This need is clearly seen in news coverage, which one has every chance of seeing in reports from conflicts and wars in the former Yugoslavia and the former Soviet Union. The danger of news coverage on TV, however, is that the events are presented so briefly that any stance we take will be absurdly superficial, something which can have disastrous consequences. There is a twofold problem here. On the one hand, adopting a responsible stance means that one does not only understand the violent actions resulting from a conflict, which is what the news media focus on. One also has to understand the matter involved, the situation in which the perpetrators of outrages find themselves, and lastly what sort of people they are – an understanding of man is only part of the understanding necessary for ethically responsible action. On the other hand, we live a finite life and in practically all cases will never gain more than a superficial knowledge of local or global events. To a great extent we live with half-baked opinions, loose assumptions and inadequate understanding. This dilemma should encourage us to be reticent in making moral judgments, but it has no general solution.

The demand for understanding or for humanity is of crucial importance in all forms of upbringing. Lack of understanding leads to one becoming blunted, and the blunted person is completely at a loss in ethical contexts. The foundation is laid in early childhood, with moral precepts being more or less a waste of time for blunted people. They are more or less hopeless victims of any influence coming from films of violence, war reports, etc. To put it another way: if I am right in my claims, then the problem is not so much the vast amount of violence shown to children and young people as the ballast with which they meet these things: how much they are able to identify with the victims, show sympathetic insight into and share other people's feelings, understand what fear, horror and powerlessness really are.

Seen from the point of view of ethics – as well as of the quality of life – the development of understanding and feelings is crucial. This is a hard formative task, but a royal road is involvement in art, i.a. because it gives one access to the feelings, experiences and the world of others which we rarely achieve, as well as to that which is strange and other.

Ethics without understanding

Lack of any sense of the importance of understanding for ethics is typical of the formalistic forms of ethics. It is of course Kant, though also classical utilitarianism, insofar as it regards the principle of utility as a valid law in itself, which can everywhere be used as a scientific lawfulness, without application having any consequence for the principle itself.

As I drew attention to at the outset, this comprehension contains an illusion. Not only does all of ethics demand participation of understanding; understanding of the ethical principles is also developed via their use. By nature ethics is applied ethics, something it also was from antiquity more or less up to Kant. The relation between ethical principles and their use differs from that between natural laws and their use. It is only by trying to realize such commandments as *Thou shalf not steal* that one understands its full import, as well perhaps as its limitations. What can one say, for example, about the many people whose only opportunity of getting hold of the necessary means of sustaining life is by stealing? The same thing applies to *Thou shalt not lie*. An understanding of this commandment is developed via situations where, for example, one has been unfaithful to one's partner and has had to consider whether truth or lying is the best solution, where one has had to choose between truth and one's job, or where one has had to console a relative who is terminally ill.

Kant was criticized as early as by Hegel for his formalism, the discussion resurfacing, for example, concerning Habermas' discourse ethics. Habermas principle of discourse ethics is a communicative, or dialogic, variant of Kant's categorical imperative. Hegel's objections to Kant have therefore been resuscitated in the critique of Habermas[9].

Here, though, I would like to draw attention to an other side of the problem. It is possible to maintain that pure principle ethics has a touch of the inhuman. Peter Railton even talks about alienation[10]. If I justify taking my partner into consideration by saying that it is after all my duty to act in such a way, or that the good is the greatest possible happiness for most people, she would be justified in feeling degraded, since my consideration has nothing to do with her as a person and my feelings for her. Railton's argument can be cited in support of the point of view that if one ignores understanding, i.e. reduces ethics to the second layer, this leads to inhumanity and to a form of alienation. That is perhaps impossible to avoid in certain situations, where one's actions affect many people, as is typical of political actions, but it must nevertheless be insisted on that ethics has to do with taking others into consideration, not with living up to principles or norms.

Ethical principles cannot be compared with a body of laws, in either the legal or scientific sense. They have more the nature of pieces of good advice that anyone may embrace and use with understanding and insight. Even so they differ from ordinary advice by the binding force of the ethical words *good, ought*, etc. and by the accompanying sanctions.

Understanding without ethics, or the problem of consciousness-raising

Ethics cannot do without understanding. Although one could on the other hand ask whether understanding could do without ethics. In other words, whether a sufficiently full understanding of a situation, an event, a person would by itself lead to right action. The problem can also be formulated slightly differently. Understanding in the broad sense also includes consciousness-raising. It is scarcely reasonable to characterize all understanding as being consciousness-raising, but it is nevertheless a form of understanding. The concept of consciousness-raising has been particularly influenced by Hegel; here, however, I am using it only to mean: a committed or integrated arrival at insight into relations that are of significant value or meaning. Integration or commitment mean that the personality as a whole, with its identity, is involved in the understanding. Consciousness-raising will often have the character of a process in which one experiences, e.g. experiences the nature of love and sexuality, or experiences power relations in society. Consciousness-raising is closely related to the concept of *Bildung*[11]. The question can then be put another way: can the raising of consciousness by itself lead to right action?

Socrates said it could, insofar as he claimed that virtue is knowledge, and he understands knowledge as being precisely integrated understanding. This way of thinking is found once again in Hegel, and the Socratic answer appears in the Hegelian tradition as a theme with variations. The various versions this way of thinking acquires in the Marxist and existentialist traditions I do not intend to pursue here.

I do not however believe that this point of view is a tenable one. As long as I have not made the issue more precise the discussion will of course be rather woolly. But let me put it another way: consciousness-raising has presumably a tendency to give rise to that which is good and right, since the more fully one understands an event, an action or a person, the greater the probability is that one understands in the sense of accepting, and that one feels oneself involved as regards responsibility. There can scarcely be any doubt that consciousness-raising in general promotes tolerance and awareness of responsibility.

On the other hand neither tolerance nor awareness of responsibility by themselves have an answer to how one ought to act. Instructions for action in the shape of concrete values, attitudes or norms are something else and must be justified in another way. One can argue on the basis of experience from the history of philosophy as follows: if we assume that the great ethicists of the history of philosophy have all been conscious of the problems and potential of the ethical life, then the philosophical discussion of the basic ethical principles shows that consciousness-raising by itself does not lead to certain content-filled principles. Nor is there any agreement within the Hegelian tradition about the content of ethics. Perhaps one ought to add that instructions for action in the shape of content-filled ethical principles are indispensable in everyday life. If philosophy, understood as the realization of reason, finds that it is not its concern, then it misunderstands its own source, which consists precisely of general problems as they arise in all other kinds of occupations. At the same time it also leaves material ethical considerations and decisions to chance – or to that which is worse still.

The demand for understanding

We are always already involved in understanding. It is not an activity brought about by ethics, since it is quite simply a part of what it means to be a human being. Every action or thought manifests one or more forms of understanding. Driving a car is a manifestation of understanding how to drive, just as research is a manifestation of understanding how to use language, symbols, a laboratory, or whatever. Understanding is in a sense closely related to competence.

Ethics, however, cannot be content with this general everyday kind of understanding. In terms of ethics understanding also becomes a demand. This is because understanding forms the basis for moral judgment and action, which can never be better than their own basis. In complicated cases in particular the work of understanding can be absolutely crucial. To add a couple more examples: adopting a stance and acting in relation to a judicial settlement in the former communist countries or to a murder case in an immigrant family is utterly dependent on having an indepth understanding of the matter. It is easy to pass judgment on the basis of superficial knowledge, but it is unjust or unethical.

What is demanded of the individual is not that he should lay aside his subjectivity, but, on the contrary, that he should use it in a particular way. Understanding does not come about in 'a cool hour', if by this one means a disengaged, dispassionate situation. On the other hand, passions and interests can distort understanding. There is a saying that love makes blind. But it is equally justifiable to claim that one sees by virtue of love. Both claims have a core of truth. So the task is to define more closely the conditions that allow understanding to become enlightenment, as well as the conditions that allow distortion to take place[12].

So the ethical demand for understanding must be: use your humanity as wholly and fully as you can before making ethical decisions. It is a demand for sympathetic insight, imagination and understanding in the narrow sense. The last-mentioned means that one ought to seek as complete and objective or true understanding of matter, situation, persons and actions as possible. An understanding of actions has to do both with the actions on which one has to take a stance and with the possibilities one has to convert one's understanding stance into action, including the consideration of possible alternative avenues of action. But truth is only part of the demand made of the total understanding. One could say that the full demand consists of impartial, existential committed enlightenment.

The demand for understanding is partially a demand made of the acting person, but it is also a demand to all those involved in upbringing and to all institutions in society: promote the humanity of the individual. It is especially important that children and young people have opportunities for developing their humanity, as frustrations within this area can damage them morally for the rest of their lives.

Dividing ethics into two layers, that of the understanding and of true ethics, is somewhat schematic. In fact we also understand by virtue of moral and ethical pre-conceptions and pre-judgments. Which implies at least that the two layers are often interwoven. However, all ethical pre-judgments, like all other presuppositions, can take on the nature of prejudices in the negative sense of the term. It is a justifiable demand to try and separate them and neutralize them insofar as one is trying to achieve an impartial understanding. Nor are we talking about a separation of a descriptive and a normative layer in ethics, by the way. As has been shown, the demand to make right use of one's understanding is an ethical demand. Moreover, true ethics is full of description. Discussions of what such concepts as love, solidarity, courage, uprightness, trust, and their opposites, are will include both normative and descriptive characteristics.

The ethics of understanding is much more comprehensive than true ethics. In situations which do not require taking an ethical stance in the real sense one can act solely on the basis of understanding. However, it remains a demand that one uses one's understanding as well as possible. So one might be tempted to argue that the ethics of understanding applies to every situation, as opposed to true ethics. But that be misleading, even so. A large number of everyday situations smack of routine and therefore only require a routine understanding. A real demand for understanding only applies when opposition has to be overcome, when the action requires an effort, when one is faced with the unusual, strange or absurd. In many contexts the demand for understanding is synonymous with using one's professional competence to the best of one's ability. Professional carelessness, whether it has to do with building, an academic dissertation or a work of art, is also an ethical problem.

The moral point of view

The question as to why a moral consideration should be applied at all must be asked of the two layers of ethics separately. Firstly, the traditional question as to why one should involve oneself in an ethical consideration at all.

The managing of power and dependency relations is part of all communication between people, no matter what the content of that communication otherwise is. One can reject concrete possibilities to be given power, but by acting one cannot decide not to take part in the basic exercising of power. By one's actions one therefore contributes to affecting the happiness and unhappiness of others, to shaping their lives and destinies. Time and again we make a mess of things, create unwanted unhappiness and suffering, cause the good things in life and the burdens to be unequally distributed and thereby become involved in questions of showing consideration. Clarifying the problem and assuming it mean precisely adding a moral view.

The problem is made more acute by the fact that we are already entangled in other people's lives. Self-interest and an interest in the welfare of others cannot be easily kept apart. My happiness and unhappiness are intimately linked to my children's – everything I do for them I do collectively for my own sake and for theirs[13]. So the problem is not why one should show consideration for others than oneself, but how one is to prioritize consideration to the various parties in the communication in relation to each other.

The understanding point of view

It can also correspondingly be said about understanding that it too is something one is always at work on, something with which one is involved in one's surroundings, other people, things and matters. The basic ethical demand for understanding is, as already mentioned, impartial, committed enlightenment. So the question is: why?

It is an extensive problem – I intend to restrict myself to interpersonal relations. The answer is the same as before: I already always find myself within a horizon of understanding, always have a certain understanding of others, one that is constantly being extended. Every act of communication has an expressive side and every expression starts a process of understanding in me, unnoticed for most of the time. In meeting another person I immediately sense a great deal about that person, mainly because of expressive behaviour, something Doris Lessing's work is one long illustration of[14]. Every person's view of other people probably includes everything from well-established truths to loose and completely mistaken opinions. Like so much else in our life-world.

Understanding in human communication takes place constantly and involuntarily. We are already always an illuminating force in our own world, in the process of separating illusion and reality, the partial and the impartial, the false from the true. Clarifying this and accepting the problem means assuming understanding as an ethical task.

Immorality, amorality and the evil of innocence

It would be tempting to say that the setting aside of the truly ethical demands leads to immorality, the setting aside of the demands for understanding to amorality. But things are not that simple. Immorality is a setting aside of otherwise accepted moral principles. The immoral person knows somewhere deep down that he or she is doing that which is wrong. Amorality on the other hand is a lack of understanding for morality at all or a conscious denial of it.

One can be immoral both in relation to the ethical demands as to the demands for understanding. One does the wrong thing one knows one ought not to do. In a corresponding way one can be amoral at both levels. Ethical amorality can be a conscious setting aside of any mention of ethics – the nihilist, as exemplified in Dostoevsky's novels. The ethical amoralist may also be the person for whom morality is a closed country. But the question is whether this is always due to a lack of understanding of moral words and concepts, thereby being linked to an amorality of understanding.

In the same way amorality of the understanding can be a conscious setting aside of the demand for humanity, as well as a lack of, or defective, humanity. Nietzsche is perhaps an example of the former. Consistently applied this point of view is self-destructive both in theory and in practice.

The latter, defects in humanity, can assume various different forms. Let me name just two of them. Even though one lacks understanding for other people, it is possible to accept a codified morality and to act mechanically in accordance with it. It looks like morality and it works, insofar as motivation is irrelevant for the observance of principles. But in actual fact it is a pitiless doctrinarianism. It could be called the lunacy of obligation. Is it immoral or amoral? In my opinion it is the latter.

A second form results from certain people being unable to show sympathetic insight into and to share the joys and sorrows of others. Such a lack can crop up from time to time for all of us, but here I am thinking of people for whom this is a more recurrent characteristic. We are dealing here with egocentrism, something which can be seen in cynics as well as artists, who live in a certain sense off their self-centredness. Such people can cause quite a lot of evil without realizing it, or without being in a position to realize it. In a way one could speak of the evil of innocence.

Translated by John Irons

Notes
1. Cf. *Den etiske fordring* and *Norm og Spontaneitet*. Consult the list of literature concerning translations of the Danish texts.
2. These basic views are enlarged upon and sought to be justified in my book *Communicative Ethics in Theory and Practice*, which is also my point of departure for some of the following.
3. Understanding as a concept has primarily been dealt with within the German hermeneutical tradition. The following is specially based on Heidegger: *Sein und Zeit §31 et passim* and Gadamer: *Wahrheit und Methode*.
4. K. E. Løgstrup: *Vidde og prægnans*, p. 29ff and p. 64f.

5. *'Sache', 'sachlich'* and *'Sachlichkeit'* are basic concepts for Gadamer's hermeneutics, something which is not clearly revealed in the English edition of *Truth and Method*, where the three words are not consistently translated and the relationship between them not marked.
   Here *'matter'* is a translation of the German *'Sache'* (Danish *'sag'*), *'matter-of-fact'* of *'sachlich'* (Danish *'saglig'*), which means both that which pertains to a matter and that which is in accordance with a matter, i.e. true, objective. *'Matter-of-factness'* is a translation of *'Sachlichkeit'* (Danish *'saglighed'*).
6. H.-G. Gadamer: *Wahrheit und Methode*, p. 278f.
7. Cf. Kierkegaard: *Afsluttende Uvidenskabeligt Efterskrift* [Concluding Unscientific Postscript], Part II, Section II, Chapter 2 *(Collected Works* Vol. VII, p. 157ff).
8. Kierkegaard: *Sygdommen til Døden* [The Sickness unto Death], *(Collected Works* Vol. XI, p. 161ff).
9. See *Moralität und Sittlichkeit. Das Problem Hegels und die Diskursethik*, publ. by W. Kuhlmann, Frankfurt 1986. Cf. also my discussion of this subject in *Communicative Ethics in Theory and Practice*, Ch. 4.
10. Peter Railton: Alienation, Consequentialism, and the Demands of Morality, in S. Scheffler (ed.): *Consequentialism and its Critics*, Oxford 1988. Sartre made the same critique in a vigorous attack on Kant's ethics of duty in *Cahiers pour une morale*, pp 277 – 85. Cf. also K.E. Løgstrup: The Exaggeration of the importance of Principles in Moral Reasoning, *Man and World*, Vol. I/3, pp. 412-27.
11. Cf. Gadamer: *Wahrheit und Methode*, p. 7ff.
12. Habermas has made a contribution with his theory concerning supremacy relations of a social and mental nature that distort supremacy-free communication, cf. i.a. *Der Universalitätsanspruch der Hermeneutik*.
13. Cf. also K.E. Løgstrup: *Den etiske fordring*, Chapter VII, section 2, and Railton, op. cit., p. 127f.
14. Cf. also Allport: Pattern and Growth in Personality, p. 469ff.

Bibliography:
Allport, G. W., 1961: *Pattern and Growth in Personality*, Holt, Rinehart and Winston, New York.
Apel, Karl-Otto *et al.*, 1971: *Hermeneutik und Ideologiekritik*, Suhrkamp, Frankfurt.
Gadamer, Hans-Georg,1960: *Wahrheit und Methode*, J. C. B. Mohr, Tübingen.
–, 1975: *Truth and Method*, The Seabury Press, New York (trans. of Gadamer 1960).
Habermas, Jürgen, 1976: *Was heißt Universalpragmatik?* In: Apel, 1976.
–, 1981: *Theorie des kommunikativen Handelns 1-2*, Suhrkamp, Frankfurt.
–, 1983: Diskursethik – Notizen zu einem Begründungsprogram, in: *Moralbewußtsein und kommunikatives Handeln*, Suhrkamp, Frankfurt.
–, 1986: Moralität und Sittlichkeit. Treffen Hegels Einwände gegen Kant auch auf die Diskursethik zu? in: W. Kuhlmann 1986.
Heidegger, Martin, 1927: *Sein und Zeit*, Max Niemeyer, Tübingen.
–, 1962: *Being and Time*, London (trans. of Heidegger 1927).
Kierkegaard, Søren, *Samlede Værker* [Collected Works], I-XIV, 1st ed. Copenhagen 1901-06. The pages of this edition is given in the English standard edition:
–, *Kierkegaards Writings*, i – XXV, Princeton University Press, 1978-. Ed. by Hovard H. Hong.
Kuhlmann, W (ed), 1986: *Moralität und Sittlichkeit*, Suhrkamp, Frankfurt a. M.
Løgstrup, K. E., 1956: *Den etiske fordring*, Gyldendal, Copenhagen, trans. as
–, 1971: *The Ethical Demand*, Fortress Press, Philadelphia.

–, 1968: The Exaggeration of the Importance of Principles in Moral Reasoning, *Man and World*, Vol. 1/3, pp. 412-27.
–, 1972: *Norm og spontaneitet*, Gyldendal, Copenhagen, enlarged and trans. as
–, 1989: *Norm und Spontaneität*, J. C. B. Mohr, Tübingen
–, 1976: *Vidde og prægnans, Sprogfilosofiske betragtninger, Metafysik I*, Gyldendal, Copenhagen, trans. as:
–, 1991: *Weite und Prägnanz*, J. C. B. Mohr, Tübingen.
Railton, Peter, 1988: Alienation, Consequentialism, and the Demands of Morality, in: Scheffler, 1988, pp. 93-133.
Sartre, Jean-Paul (1983): *Cahiers pour une morale*, Gallimard, Paris
Scheffler, Samuel (ed.), 1988: *Consequentialism and its Critics*, Oxford University Press.
Thomassen, Niels, 1992a: *Communicative Ethics in Theory and Practice*, Macmillan, London and New York.
–, 1992b: *Filosofisk impressionisme. Temaer i K. E. Løgstrups filosofi [Philosophical Impressionism. Themes in the Philosophy of K. E. Løgstrup]*, Gyldendal, Copenhagen.

THE METAETHICAL FOUNDATIONS OF HUMAN RIGHTS[1]

Erich Klawonn

Department of Philosophy
University of Southern Denmark

I

From a philosophical point of view, it is quite obvious that the idea of universal human rights[2] must rely on presuppositions of a metaethical nature.

The most important of these presuppositions is the possibility of an objective or absolute ethics, i.e. a system of moral truths which are valid in themselves, independently of changing individual or collective attitudes and opinions.

In contemporary metaethical thinking this presupposition is quite often rejected, leaving the idea of universal human rights without any foundation. Even today it is a dominant metaethical view that moral judgements are expressions of feelings or attitudes, and that there is therefore no such thing as moral truths (at least not in the ordinary sense of the word truth) – and by implication no truths about human rights.

I do, however, believe, that such 'scepticist' views of the nature of morality are fundamentally wrong, and that it is in fact possible to provide a rational foundation of the idea of universal human rights. In order to demonstrate this, I will now outline a defence of an absolutistic metaethical theory which could serve as a foundation of human rights.[3]

First of all, I wish to draw attention to a level in our moral intuitions which we may call *enlightened moral common sense*. This is a level of morality which has a certain authoritative status with regard to philosophical theories of ethics, as we tend to reject such theories if they have 'morally absurd' consequences.

As an example, it can be mentioned that it is generally regarded as a difficulty for *classical utilitarianism,* which operates on *the principle of the greatest happiness of the greatest number*, that it seems to follow from this theory that the ancient Romans did the right thing by letting humans be killed by lions in order to entertain the masses (the point being that the discomfort of a small number is outweighed by the total sum of pleasure of a large number). We do not just take such a conclusion *ad notam*. We regard it as unacceptable – which may either lead to a rejection of classical utilitarianism or to attempts to show that it does not, after all, have the aforementioned consequence.

Another example is an objection to the Kantian doctrine of *The Categorical Imperative*. According to Kant, it follows from the theory of The Categorical Imperative that it can never be morally correct to tell a lie – which would imply that somebody who, say, during World War II, was hiding Jews in his cellar, and was asked about this issue by the Gestapo, was not entitled to tell a lie. The most he could do was not say anything – which would have the same consequences as telling the truth, since it would invite to a closer investigation. Once again, we do not just take this conclusion *ad notam*. We either reject or modify the ethical theory, or we attempt to show that it does not, after all, have the consequence in question.

These examples lend support to the view that some of our moral intuitions are so firm and stable that we tend to reject any theory which contradicts them. Here it should of course also be noted that morality is not the product of a theory of ethics. It is a phenomenon which exists before theories of ethics, and which such theories are about. Therefore it is quite natural that pre-given moral intuitions may serve as a criterion of the validity of theories about the nature of morality.

It is of course obvious that not all kinds of moral intuitions are equally suited for the role as an instance of court in relation to theories of ethics. The moral wrongness of unusual sexual activities may well have been common sense during a certain historical period – but this kind of common sense could hardly serve as a criterion for the validity of philosophical theories of ethics. On the other hand, the view that it is morally wrong to kill or mutilate other people for the fun of the thing seems to be an intuition of a more firm and stable nature. We could not easily adopt the view that our verdict on this issue is just an expression of a cultural prejudice – and that a correct theory of ethics could therefore imply the moral acceptability or even the praiseworthiness of such an act.

Therefore, it is central metaethical issue to supply a foundation of a kind of enlightened moral common sense which may also serve as a basis of universal human rights – which is, however, not the same thing as providing an argument for all kinds of moral common sense.

II

In the following I shall attempt to show that enlightened moral common sense – as opposed to ordinary common sense – can be rationally reconstructed on the basis of three elements: *prima facie value, rational administration of value* and *empathy*.

In order to substantiate this contention, the nature of the aforementioned 3 elements should be taken into consideration.

The term *prima facie value* refers to positive or negative value-characters within the lifeworld – or (to introduce what I regard as a useful technical term) 'the own-sphere' – of an experiencing individual. *Pain* is an example of a prima facie negative value, *pleasure* is an example of a prima facie positive value. They are, properly speaking, only prima facie values, because they can be relativized or annulled by a further value context. For instance, under normal circumstances the pain of dental treatment can be tolerated as a means to avoid prolonged toothache, and some pleasures should be avoided because they lead to pain and frustration in the long run. In my view, *value proper* is a kind of prima facie value which is not annulled or relativized by a further value-context. For the sake of convenience (and in so far as it does not tend to cause confusion), I do, however, often use the term value as a designation of both value proper and prima facie value.

In this connection I wish to direct attention to a phenomenon, which we may call *value-pressure* or *the imperativity of value*.[4] A proper understanding of this phenomenon may lead to an understanding of the nature of rational administration of value and, in a wider perspective, to an understanding of the specific moral nature of certain types of rational administration of value.

Let us consider an example of simple, prima facie negative value – *pain*. What makes pain a negative value-character is the fact that, as part of its own nature, it contains a certain *aversive* aspect. Pain is not a phenomenon which in the first place exists in a neutral manner, and which subsequently obtains a prima facie negative value by being subjected to an attitude of antipathy or aversion. On the contrary, it is part of the very nature of pain that it has a character of (prima facie) undesirability, which involves an imperativity or 'pressure' towards its own elimination. Pain is in itself, according to its own nature, and all other things being equal, *disagreeable* (hereby it is of course not denied that pain may assume an agreeable quality by being associated with pleasure, but in that case the pain is not considered in a pure form or in isolation). Correspondingly, a positive value-character has an inherent, immediate (or prima facie) desirability, which implies a 'pressure' towards acquisition or preservation. Therefore, the prima facie aversive nature of pain and the prima facie desirable nature of pleasure are not caused by an attitude. It is rather the cause of an attitude and consequently of a tendency to action in a certain direction. In other words: pain tends (typically) towards eliciting an attitude of aversion and corresponding actions, while pleasure tends towards eliciting an attitude of sympathy or liking which naturally leads to corresponding actions. It seems reasonable to assume that something similar applies to all kinds of value-phenomena (even to instrumental values due to their relation to primary values).

To avoid misunderstanding, it should be mentioned that though some value-characters – e.g. pain and pleasure – are given as inner states of the subject, value-characters may also be phenomenologically objective in the sense that they are experienced as desirable or aversive properties of objects in the lifeworld. Beauty and ugliness are examples of such phenomenologically objective value-properties. Whether the properties in question are *ontologically* objective is, however, another question that must, in my opinion, be answered in the negative.

Given the correctness of the view that value-characters possess an inherent imperativity or that they exert 'pressure' in a certain direction, we may introduce a notion of *selfish, practical rationality*, or rational administration of value with regard to the own-sphere – i.e. with regard to the lifeworld as experienced from one's own point of view.

It is prima facie rational to procure positive value and to eliminate negative value. The nature of, say, intense pain is such that it provides its victim with a prima facie good reason to avoid it or get rid of it, whereas the nature of intense pleasure is such that it represents a prima facie good reason to preserve it or to get hold of it. Here we are talking about 'practical rationality' only in a momentary or synchronic perspective. But rational administration of value also takes the time factor into account. *A basic principle of practical rationality is that present and future value-characters should be regarded as being of equal importance*, provided that there are no other relevant differences. According to this principle, the pain that I experience today and the pain that I am going to experience tomorrow are – all other things equal – on a par. And furthermore: due to differences in degree, future value-characters may outweigh present value-characters. Therefore it may e.g. be rational to accept a certain amount of momentary negative value in order to avoid a larger amount of negative value or perhaps to achieve a large amount of positive value in the future.

The possibility of comparisons of value – e.g. positive and negative – rest on the principle that *degrees of value are identical with or resultant from degrees of value-pressure and can be known as such.* We may for instance assume that the amount of positive value required to counterbalance a certain amount of negative value can in most cases be decided by means of an intuitive comparison of the relative imperativity or degrees of 'value-pressure' of the value-characters in question.

Hereby we have established the outlines of a theory of *quality of life* or *value-administration in a selfish perspective.* According to this theory, choices which lead to a dominance of positive value (considered as such only according to degrees of positive value-pressure within the own-sphere) through time are in fact *better* or *more rational* in a selfish perspective than choices which lead to a dominance of negative value (where the degree of negativity is equivalent to the degree of negative value-pressure within the own-sphere). That a life of happiness and fulfilment is preferable to a life of pain and frustration is not just a matter of taste. The concrete experiences which constitute the content of the categories of happiness or frustration may differ, e.g. at different times or with regard to different individuals. What is positive value for me today and tomorrow or for me and for you may be quite different things. *But that does not in any way affect the validity of the 'meta-value' of increasing positive value and decreasing negative value.*

In other words: though concrete values may be relative, the validity of the supraordinate ideal of value-optimization is absolute and therefore independent of subjective and cultural contingencies. If I hate the taste of oysters, whereas you love it, it would contribute to value-optimization in your lifeworld (or own-sphere) to eat oysters, whereas to avoid the very same thing would contribute to value-optimization in mine. And if modern poetry exerts an irresistible attraction on you, whereas I find it boring, I have no quarrel with you. Such differences do not in any way affect the supraordinate ideal of practical, selfish rationality in the form of value-optimization (whatever that may be) within one's own lifeworld or own-sphere. It may well be the case that some preferences are common to all or most human beings, whereas others differ – but that is irrelevant in this context.

To anticipate questions of ethical – as opposed to selfish – administration of value, it is interesting to note that if value-optimization with regard to all own-spheres were accepted as a supraordinate moral ideal, it would lead to a good deal of tolerance in matters of ethics. This is because the main limitation imposed on behaviour would be the equal right of value-optimization of all own-spheres, whereas all specific value preferences would be regarded as *prima facie* acceptable. We shall, however, return to the question of moral value-administration below.

To sum up: At this point we have established 3 basic points: (1) The occurrence of value characters within the own-sphere or individual lifeworld. (2) The fact that the imperativity or value-pressure of value-characters provides a good reason to avoid negative value and to procure or preserve positive value. And (3): The principle that for selfish reasons, future value-characters should be regarded as being *in principle* on a par with present value characters. Hereby we have – in brief outline – established a norm of selfish, rational administration of value which seems to be trans-subjectively and trans-culturally valid. What counts as positive and negative value may well be relative to individuals and cultural settings, but the ideal of value-optimization with regard to the own-sphere remains constant if we only take selfish interests into account. (It should, however, be recalled that such interests may well, as according to Aristotle, include social interests).

In this context is should, of course, also be noted that these points concerning rational administration of value with regard to the own-sphere are consequences of the first two of the basic constituents of enlightened moral common sense – *value and rationality*. Thus we have (though of course only in broad outline) arrived at an 'ethics' in the sense of Greek antiquity, i.e. a theory of welfare for oneself or quality of life, but not at theory of unselfish or 'other-directed' administration of value, which is the meaning of ethics or morality in the modern sense.

Such historical fluctuations in the meaning of a word do not, however, prove that the different phenomena denoted by it do not exist or are of a purely 'historical' nature. The nature of unselfish administration of value may well – as I will attempt to show – be something that exists in its own right and has a nature which is independent of cultural and subjective contingencies.

III

In order to pass beyond the level of selfish administration of value, it is necessary to introduce the third element in the attempted reconstruction of enlightened moral common sense: *empathy or empathic identification*.

I shall not elaborate on the causal background of empathy. It should only be noted that in the present context the term *empathy* is used as a name of the mode of access which an individual field of experience has to other such fields of experience. Empathy is the mental function which renders the lifeworlds or own-spheres of other individuals (which I propose to call *the other-sphere*) present to oneself. To express the same thing in a more precise manner: *empathy is the function which creates a representation of the other-sphere within the own-sphere*. In this sense the actual occurrence and the degrees of empathy in different situations are of course empirical facts. But the notion of empathy also has a cognition-founding or (in the sense of Kant) *transcendental* significance, as it is a condition for the existence of a whole cognitive dimension – *knowledge of others*. In this connection we may talk about *a transcendental minimum of empathy* without which other sentient creatures could not be experienced and known as such.

It seems natural to assume that empathy is a necessary condition for both human sociality and morality. If not even a transcendental or knowledge-founding minimum of empathy is present (like when a lion attacks and eats another animal), moral categories like good and evil, right and wrong appear to be inapplicable. In such cases we are obviously dealing with morally neutral phenomena of nature. But given that empathic cognition is present, the use of such categories lies near at hand. If, say, a certain sub-species (a mutation, perhaps) of lions has a complete empathic cognition of the feelings of the antelopes that they eat, it would be tempting to view their behaviour as morally problematic (though they may perhaps be excused, since other conditions for morality, for instance rationality and freedom of choice, may be absent).

The ethically important aspect of the empathic relation is that it transfers value-pressure from the other-sphere to the own-sphere, so that value-characters in another field of experience become relevant to oneself. Thus, a high degree of empathy may make another person's suffering intolerable to oneself – which would of course provide a compelling motive to help that person. And in a similar manner, a high degree of empathy may render another person's happiness almost or even just as desirable as one's own, so that one is strongly motivated to act in order to make that person happy. In such cases the empathic relation creates a kind of *protoethical relation* to others (i.e. other people and even other sentient creatures). This relation does not amount to morality in the strict sense, since the actions that it prompts cannot be clearly distinguished from selfish value-administration. It may be just as disagreeable to ignore empathically introduced value-experiences of others as to ignore value-characters that strictly belong to oneself. It can also be mentioned that in many cases protoethical reactions tend to be quite capricious, as they depend on momentary power-relations between on the one hand value-characters originating in the own-sphere and on the other empathically represented other-sphere values. Such protoethical reactions can, however, be viewed as a kind of preliminaries to morality. It can also be mentioned that in the sphere of close relations we find stable protoethical relations which are more similar to morality in the strict sense than simple protoethical reactions are. The nature of the relation to one's children, spouse or close friends is usually such that one is disposed to provide comfort and care even in situations where one's momentary level of empathy is relatively low. But still such reactions do not differ much from selfish administration of value, since even in a selfish perspective it may in many cases be the best policy to act as though a high degree of empathy is present, even if it is not. I may perhaps be momentarily inclined to ignore my crying child – but if I did so, the consequences might well turn out to be quite disagreeable to myself.

In order to understand the difference between protoethics and ethics (or morality) proper, it is important to note that, as with other kinds of cognition, empathy has a certain 'self-transcending nature' (which should not be confused with its transcendental or knowledge-founding nature).

The self-transcending nature of empathy can be explained as follows:

Cognition requires a mode of access. In order for empathic cognition to reach out towards the real existence of others, i.e. towards a state of affairs which is different from the act of cognition itself, it must contain the aspect of 'a self-transcending nature'. It must, in other words, represent the other-sphere as having an independent and definite character of its own, to which the empathic relation provides a more or less accurate approximation. Thus, in the case of empathic cognition, the other-sphere is experienced by me as existing in and for itself and as being whatever it is independently of whether I experience it or not.

These observations concerning the empathic relation between the own-sphere and the other-sphere may pave the way for an understanding of the nature of morality proper.

IV

As mentioned above, empathy may generate an immediate impulse to benefit others – which is a phenomenon that is somewhat similar to morality, but still of a pre-moral or protoethical nature. But imagine that a person chooses help a suffering fellow-being without being explicitly prompted to do so because of the relative strengths (or value pressure) of value-characters within his own-sphere, or by considerations pertaining to value-optimization within the own-sphere. *In that case the person's behaviour falls under the heading of ethics or morality proper, as it is, in a clear sense, unselfish.*

To express this in a more precise manner, it is my contention that in the case of a strictly moral action two conditions are fulfilled: (1) the independent existence and nature of the other-sphere is recognized, i.e. it is recognized as being what it is in and for itself, in its own perspective; and (2) its immanent value-characters are treated as exerting a demand of recognition and if necessary help and care from oneself, no matter whether the empathic relation introduces such a degree of value-pressure that for selfish reasons it would be the best policy not to ignore it. In other words: *The essence of morality proper consists in one's recognition of the value-perception of the other-sphere as being relevant to one's own actions, even if no pronounced empathic bond is present.*

The possible relevance of this motive is introduced by the very cognition of other sentient creatures combined with the idea of rational administration of value already introduced with regard to the own-sphere. Hereby we arrive at *the idea of a possible other-directed, rational administration of value*. This idea represents a norm (e.g. in the sense that it is possible to conform to it or deviate from it through one's actions), which is equivalent to an elementary notion of a *moral demand.*

In order to understand this, it should be noted that the transcendental minimum of empathy always introduces *some degree of motivating force* into the own-sphere. Considered in a pure form, or on its own terms, the aforementioned norm 'demands' (i.e. exerts imperativity towards) conformity with it. *Morality motivates* – otherwise it would not be relevant to our actions. But since other motivating factors may also be present, 'the moral motive' (i.e. the idea of a possible rational administration of value with regard to the other-sphere) may not be dominant within the total field of value-experiences. *But it can be made dominant by means of a free choice*. It is the execution of this free choice which is the mark of morality proper.

The following example may serve to illustrate the difference between advanced protoethics and morality proper:

If my child is in distress, and I do not do my best the help her, my administration of value is probably deficient even on selfish premises. If, however, I find a stranger lying on the street with a broken leg, and my level of empathy is relatively low, it may well be the case that I could, without any serious selfish repercussions, choose to ignore him – but I could, of course, also choose to help him (for instance by calling an ambulance). In this case my reaction would be a question of ethics or morality.

According to the views presented above, a certain freedom of choice regarding one's own moral level is an essential part of the nature of morality. I may choose to ignore the suffering of my fellow-beings, or even, if I am so disposed, to increase it. But the norm which determines *the moral level* of one's actions – i.e. the norm of other-directed, rational administration of value – is constant, since it follows from the very cognition of the other-sphere as another own-sphere with the same immanent claim to rational administration of value as oneself. In that sense the norm of other-directed, rational administration of value is *absolute*. It is, so to speak, the measure of good and evil, since it is what so-called good people freely conform to and what so-called bad or evil people freely deviate from.

Hereby the capricious character of protoethics is overcome, since a non-relative norm has been introduced according to which others are regarded as existing in their own right and as having the same claim to rational administration of value as oneself. Whether or not I have a high degree of empathy with a person is regarded as fortuitous and consequently without any bearing on the moral issue in question. I may, of course, choose to act in a morally reprehensible manner – but that is due to the freedom which is essential to morality proper, and not to fluctuations in the nature of the basic moral norm. The possibility of a choice between good and evil does not in any way contradict the validity of an absolute moral norm which may serve as a basis of evaluation of decisions, actions and (by implication) moral character.

In this connection it is also important to note that the norm of other-directed, rational administration of value should not be regarded as a product of a particular cultural or historical setting. It is rather a well-defined and universal motive constituted by a definite and invariable combination of transcultural conditions such as value, simple practical reason, empathy and freedom of choice in certain situations – i.e. conditions which are both knowledge-founding and necessary to the very existence of culture and sociality at a human level. Though the importance attributed to The Moral Motive may vary enormously due to individual and cultural contingencies, it is always present as a factor of potential significance to beings at a human cognitive level. In the case of such *morally qualified subjects* the norm of other-directed care is what it is and would always prevail if no conflicting motives were present.

Morality in the strict and transcultural sense can therefore be understood as a rationally mediated extension of the kind of other-directed care resulting from the protoethical relation. According to the metaethical theory which has been outlined above, *the essential characteristic of morality proper is the attempted rational administration of value with regard to others in cases where they are unable to carry out such administration themselves, and where the actual degree of emphatic identification plays no decisive role* (though the transcendental minimum of empathy must of course be present).

V

There are different levels of ethics or morality. Not only does the empathic relation combined with rationality open up the recognition of concretely encountered others as existing in their own right, i.e. as being present to themselves even in respects to which I have no immediate empathic access; it also opens up the recognition of an indefinite number of unknown others whose welfare may to some degree be affected by my actions.

Therefore we may distinguish between two different layers or levels of morality proper:

We may use the term *life-world ethics* about morality concerning individuals encountered in one's immediate surroundings, and the term *system-world ethics* about morality concerning an indefinite number of individuals outside the perceptually given lifeworld – for instance in a national or global perspective. The move towards an acceptance of moral obligations at the level of system-world ethics can be understood as a consequence of the choice to be a moral agent combined with a principle of consistency which has already been adopted when passing from protoethics to morality proper. In so far as one's actions can be known to affect the welfare of others, it is, from a rational point of view, unimportant whether the affected individuals are encountered within one's lifeworld or not.

Life-world ethics is not hereby replaced by system-world ethics. To most people the primary scene of moral action is their lifeworld – and under normal circumstances other-directed actions cannot be directly related to welfare-optimization in general. It does, however, seem reasonable to assume that there is a certain harmony or correspondence between life-world ethics and system-world ethics. Widespread ethical practice at the local level is obviously one of the most effective ways to secure welfare in general. But still, there may be conflicts between the two layers in morality proper – just as there may be conflicts between selfish administration of value and moral administration of value. Rational consideration of such conflicts must take a number of factors into account – e.g. the relative severity of the issues in question, the degree of influence that an individual agent can have on the system-world, and the number of individuals whose interests are concerned.

VI

To return to the question of the basis of universal humans rights, it seems obvious that in so far as such rights can be related to the theory of ethics presented above, they must be localized at the level of system-world ethics. In the following I shall briefly outline a defence of the view that *fundamental human rights* can in fact deduced from *The Theory of Empathy* (as we may call the metaethical theory outlined above).

All the rights mentioned in the UN-Declaration of Human Rights seem to be specifications or direct or indirect consequences of 3 fundamental types: *rights of welfare, rights of freedom* and *rights of equality.*

Since it seems reasonable to assume that rights of welfare are the most fundamental, I will comment on that type first:

Central rights of welfare are the right not to be subjected to avoidable and unnecessary suffering,[5] the right to safety and the right to satisfaction of basic needs of sustenance.[6] Obviously, such rights can be viewed as consequences of the norm of other-directed, rational administration of value – i.e. they follow directly from The Theory of Empathy.

A right to happiness is not mentioned in this connection, since the nature and pursuit of happiness are issues which are in most cases best left to the individual and cannot be subject to universal legislation. However, since happiness is the positive aspect of welfare and is in fact pursued by everybody, avoidable deprivation of the conditions of happiness is obviously a violation of a universal human right. And since the most important means to achieve happiness is the free or autonomous administration of value on the part of the individual, the right of autonomous value-administration is a fundamental *right of freedom* (i.e. apart from the fact that freedom may in itself be part of happiness). On the basis of this general right it is possible to formulate a number of particular rights of freedom with regard to different circumstances, so that we may talk of such rights in the plural.

Quite a large number of the rights mentioned in the UN-Declaration of Human Rights are mainly rights of freedom – for instance freedom from slavery, freedom of speech, freedom of thought and religion, freedom of movement and residence etc. etc.[7]

Rights of freedom are closely related or even instrumental to rights of welfare, but since this group of rights has some distinct features, we may still wish to talk of rights of freedom as a particular kind of human rights.

The first two types of right – rights of welfare and rights of freedom – are immediate and obvious consequences the metaethical theory outlined above. The third type of rights – *rights of equality* – needs some further clarification.

Rights of equality rule out various kinds of discrimination – for instance discrimination due to race, sex, colour, language, religion, political persuasion, national origin, birth and social position etc.[8] In order to understand the underlying idea of a fundamental equality between human beings (and perhaps even in some respects between human beings and animals), it should be recalled that the transcending nature of empathic cognition reveals the other-sphere as being in a certain basic respect equal to the own-sphere. The other-sphere cannot be understood otherwise than as another own-sphere, which, in its own perspective or for itself, is just as important as one's own phenomenal universe or own-sphere. Seen in its own first-person perspective an other-sphere is a total phenomenal universe, which contains all experiences, including all value-experiences, of an individual subject. Therefore we may talk of *a monadological distribution of value* – i.e. a distribution of value upon countless individual own-spheres, which relatively to one another appear as other-spheres. In so far as this fact is recognized by means of empathic cognition it leads on to the intuition of others as existing in their own right and as having the same initial claim to rational administration of value as oneself. This observation provides a kind of metaphysical foundation of the idea of an original equality between individuals and corresponding rights of equality.

VII

On the assumption that these views provide a plausible explanation of the nature of the basic categories of human rights, it seems obvious that the metaethical theory outlined above may function as a secular and rational foundation the UN-Declaration. All the rights mentioned in the Universal Declaration of Human Rights can be understood as consequences or specifications adapted to particular circumstances of *the basic rights of welfare, freedom and equality* – which for their part can be founded on the metaethical Theory of Empathy.

Though important questions (e.g. concerning conflicts, priority and specification of particular human rights) remain unanswered, it is my contention that the question of the very existence of universal human rights can be answered in the positive. This is due to the fact that the three factors (value, rationality and empathy) on which the Theory of Empathy is founded are universal conditions of human sociality and of all kinds of rational administration of value with regard to others. It is of course quite possible to deviate from the norm of rational administration of value both with regard to oneself and others. But the nature of this norm is not in itself subject to cultural or historical fluctuations. This is a fact which tends to confer a universal validity upon the most general categories of human rights, i.e. rights of welfare, freedom and equality.

These general categories may then serve as a basis of the formulation of particular rights like the ones mentioned in the Universal Declaration of Human Rights. The specification of particular rights depends on cultural and perhaps also to some extent natural contingencies such as the existence of 'institutions' like religion, marriage, the family as a fundamental unit in society, private property, the national State, legislation etc. Combined with the general categories of rights, such contingencies give rise to the formulation of specific rights that primarily concern the relations between the individual and the institutions in question.[9] But that does not in itself rule out the possibility of a general ethical foundation of what we may call *The discourse of human rights*. In this paper I have attempted to outline the possible nature of such a foundation.

Notes

1. This article is an extended version of a paper which was originally designed for oral presentation at the conference *Human Rights, Democracy and Religion*, held at The University of Southern Denmark in Odense, April 4-5 2002.
2. E.g. as according to the *Universal Declaration of Human Rights*, United Nations 1948.
3. The metaethical theory which I outline in this article has been presented in more detail in my book "Udkast til en teori om moralens grundlag" (*Sketch of a theory of the foundations of morals*), Odense University Press, 1996.
4. In *The Place of Value in a World of Facts* (1939), which has been a source of inspiration to the axiological considerations in this paper, Wolfgang Köhler uses the term 'requiredness' as a name of the phenomenon which I call *value-pressure*.

5. Cf. *Universal Declaration of Human Rights*, Article 5 et al.
6. Cf. ibid. Article 25
7. Cf. ibid. Article 13, Article 18-19 et al.
8. Cf. ibid. Article 2 et al.
9. Directly or indirectly this applies to most of the Articles in the *Universal Declaration of Human Rights* – with the possible exception of Articles 1, 3, 4 and 5.

EGALITARIANISM AND REPUGNANT CONCLUSIONS[1]

THOMAS SØBIRK PETERSEN

University of Copenhagen
Department of Education, Philosophy and Rhetoric
Njalsgade 80
2300 Copenhagen S.
E-mail: thompet@hum.ku.dk

ABSTRACT

Most philosophers discuss the Repugnant Conclusion as an objection to total utilitarianism. But this focus is one-sided. It conceals the important fact that other competing moral theories are also subject to the Repugnant Conclusion. The primary aim of this paper is to demonstrate that versions of egalitarianism are subject to the Repugnant Conclusion and other repugnant conclusions.

> They weren't only equal before God and the law. They were equal every which way. Nobody was smarter than anybody else. Nobody was better looking than anybody else. Nobody was stronger or quicker than anybody else. All equality was due to the 211th, 212th, and 213th Amendments to the Constitution, and to the unceasing vigilance of agents of the United States Handicapper General. (Kurt Vonnegut).

(i) INTRODUCTION

A principle that has attached much attention within modern normative moral philosophy is:

The Total Welfare Principle:
The best outcome is the one with the greatest total sum of welfare value

A well-known objection to this principle is the Repugnant Conclusion.

> *The Repugnant Conclusion*
> For any possible population of at least ten billion people, all with very high quality of life [population A], there must be some much larger imaginable population whose existence, if other things are equal, would be better, even though its members have lives that are barely worth living [population B].[2]

Derek Parfit believes that the Repugnant Conclusion (RC) provides firm ground on which to resist the total welfare principle of what is often called *total utilitarianism*.[3] Total utilitarianism is the normative moral theory that, besides the total welfare principle, entails the *consequentialist* component, which states that 'the right act is the act, which promotes the best outcome'.[4]

In the literature on this subject that has emerged since Parfit's objection, most philosophers discuss the RC as an objection to total utilitarianism.[5] But this focus is one-sided. It conceals the important fact that other competing moral theories are also subject to the RC.[6]

The aim of this paper is threefold. Firstly and primarily, I will demonstrate that versions of egalitarianism imply the RC and other repugnant conclusions. The repugnance of these other conclusions can be stated in terms of what in the literature is called 'The Levelling Down Objection'. Second, I want to show that egalitarianism in certain cases where the existence of individuals is contingent upon our choices cannot be subject to the Levelling Down Objection often posed against egalitarianism.[7] Finally, I want, nevertheless, to mention that egalitarianism in the above-mentioned cases is subject to an Impersonal Levelling Down Objection. A kind of Levelling Down Objection that, quite contrary to the traditional Levelling Down Objection, does not rely on the contention that some are made worse off (and no one better off) by a levelling down.

(ii) EGALITARIANISM AND REPUGNANT CONCLUSIONS

To begin with, I will briefly specify which versions of egalitarianism are the focal points of the present examination.

Equality is an important value in moral philosophy and political reasoning. But views about equality can vary according to at least two factors. There are different versions of egalitarianism depending on the *kind of equality* in question (equality before the Law, equality concerning distribution of goods or the equal importance of everyone). Most egalitarians, and indeed most normative moral philosophers are concerned with the *equal importance* of welfare. For instance, in the way that "[...] an increase in the well-being of a woman counts as much as a comparable increase in the well-being of a man, my welfare counts as neither more nor less that yours, and so on".[8] Egalitarians vary also according to the *'currency' of equality* (welfare, rights, resources etc.). In this paper, however, I want to focus on *distributive egalitarianism,* which holds that, in determining the goodness of outcomes, equality in the distribution of the good (e.g. welfare or resources) is morally relevant. Roughly speaking, the core of distributive egalitarianism (henceforth egalitarianism) is the notion that the more equality there is in the distribution of the good, the better.[9]

In order to answer the question whether egalitarianism implies the RC, I will distinguish between monistic egalitarianism and pluralistic egalitarianism and between different ways of measuring equality (or inequality).

a) Monistic egalitarianism

According to monistic egalitarianism equality is treated as the *only* morally relevant factor. Nothing else matters in the evaluation of outcomes. However, to decide whether monistic egalitarianism entails the RC depends on how to measure equality (or inequality).[10]

For most philosophers and economists the central idea is that the degree of equality in a population (or between populations) depends on how the worse off fare relative to the better off. Let's call this vaguely stated view on the measurement of equality for the Standard View (SV).[11] Monistic egalitarianism where equality is measured by the SV implies that population A and B are *equally good*, since there is perfect equality in both populations. Although this might strike many as repugnant, it cannot be as repugnant as the implication of total utilitarianism, which implies that population B is *better* than population A. So on *this* comparison between outcomes, monistic egalitarianism (combined with the SV) is not as vulnerable to the RC as total utilitarianism.

Equality can nevertheless be measured differently and thus, as we shall see, provide different answers to whether monistic egalitarianism entails the RC. Instead of measuring equality as a relation between the better and the worse off in, for instance, a population, one can measure equality according to how many relations of equality there exist in the given population. Let's call this view the Non-Standard View (NSV). The NSV is in accordance with the general idea that equality is a relationship between different people. It should now be obvious that if monistic egalitarianism is measured with the NSV, it follows that population B is preferable over population A, since there are more relations of equality in B than in A.

In sum, if monistic egalitarianism is evaluated in combination with the NSV, it will entail the RC. So on *this* comparison between outcomes, monistic egalitarianism (combined with the NSV) is as vulnerable to the RC as total utilitarianism.

However, in connection with a comparative evaluation of other outcomes than A and B, monistic egalitarianism can entail conclusions that are also repugnant. First, monistic egalitarianism would, unlike total utilitarianism, imply that two populations A and B* are *equally good,* even if the *number of people* in A and B* are the *same* – and the people in A have much more total welfare than the people in B*. Assume furthermore that the welfare is distributed equally within each outcome and that all the people in B* have lives that are worth living.[12] This is problematic. It does not seem right to claim that B* is as good as A, if every individual in A has much more welfare than every individual in B*.

Secondly, monistic egalitarians will be forced to accept, again unlike total utilitarianism, that if a population A* contains one person with a life barely above the level of all the other very well off people in A*, population B* is better than A* – assuming that the number of people in A* and B* are the same.[13]

If you believe that the RC is indeed repugnant, these implications of monistic egalitarianism might also strike you as repugnant. In other words, monistic egalitarianism entails the following repugnant conclusions:

Repugnant Conclusion* (RC*)
For any possible population (A) of at least ten billion people, all of whom have a very high quality of life, there must be some population (B*) of the same size, whose existence, if other things were equal, would be *equally good*, even though all its members have lives that are barely worth living.

Repugnant Conclusion** (RC**)
For any possible population (A*) of at least ten billion people, all of whom have a very high quality of life except one person who has an extra high quality of life, there must be some population (B*) of the same size whose existence, if other things were equal, would be *better*, even though all its members have lives that are barely worth living.

These conclusions can be claimed to be repugnant because they violate the following plausible principle:

Principle 1
Everything else being equal, if two populations A and B are of the same size, and every person in A is better off than every person in B, then A is better than B.[14]

Assume, for the discussion in this section, that the people in the populations mentioned are necessary people. Necessary people are people that have existed, exist, or will exist independently of our choices. A and B* could, for instance, be the populations of two distinct tribes in South America or different national groups in Scandinavia on the 5th of January 2004.[15]

b) Pluralistic egalitarianism

Egalitarians can, of course, be pluralists. They can claim, for instance, that population B in Parfit's objection is better than A, because B contains a larger total sum of welfare and because this additional moral factor outweighs the moral factor of equality. Hence, at least some versions of pluralistic egalitarianism imply the RC. Depending, of course, on the weight one attributes to the different values of e.g. total welfare and equality. Nevertheless, worse is to come.

Pluralistic egalitarians have to admit (i) that population A and B* are *in one relevant sense* equally good – namely, concerning equality, and (ii) that B* is *in one relevant sense* better than A* – namely, concerning equality. Again, however, these implications seem repugnant. But this is not because they imply the RC* or the RC**. The pluralist who favours total welfare as a morally relevant factor does, for one thing, not have to concede that B* and A are equally good, all things considered (or that B* is better that A*, again all things considered). However, by implying (i) and (ii) pluralistic egalitarianism violates the following further principle, which can be derived from total utilitarianism.[16]

> *Principle 2*
> Everything else being equal, if two populations A and B are of the same size, and every person in A is better off than every person in B, then A is, in any relevant sense, better than B.[17]

Assume, once again, that the people in the populations mentioned in this section are necessary people.

To further illustrate the problem of violating this principle, ask how, in any relevant respect, B* (for example) can be as good as A, if everyone in population A are better off than everyone in population B*. How can *equality* in any relevant respect make population A and B* equally good, when equality in itself does not affect the welfare of the members in these populations? By analogy, imagine two people Peter and Paul:

Peter and Paul
Peter and Paul have a very high quality of life during the first six months of 2003 (on a welfare scale from 1-10, let's say that their life in that period is on the level of 9). In the last six months of 2003 they both have a sudden and drastic decrease in their welfare because of a car accident on the 1st of July. The result of the accident is that they both in the last six months of 2003 experience a life on the level of 3 on the welfare scale.

But how could this decrease in welfare for Peter and Paul make the latter period of 2003 equally good to the former period in any relevant sense – when they are both worse off? This should go for all such equalities between people – and so for the one between A and B*.[18]

One way for egalitarians to resist this unattractive implication is to accept that equality at higher levels matters more, morally, than equality at lower levels.[19] I will not, however, pursue this strategy here.[20]

(iii) EGALITARIANISM AND THE LEVELLING DOWN OBJECTION

The objection that both monistic and pluralistic forms of egalitarianism in certain comparisons violate principle 1 and 2 can be stated in terms of the frequently proposed 'levelling down objection' (LDO) to egalitarianism.[21] For instance, egalitarianism must accept that the levelling down from A* to B*, at least in one sense is a move for the better, since this transition establishes equality between the two populations. However, before pursuing this thought, let us just go over the LDO.

Imagine two populations, A and B, of the same size. In A, the best off are at 100 and the worst off are at 50, and in B all are equally well off, though they are less well off than the members of A, say they are all at 40. According to the LDO, egalitarianism implies that the levelling down of the people in A to the level of the people in B is an improvement – at least, in one sense. But, argue adherents of the LDO, one distribution cannot be better than another distribution, if some are worse off (the A-people) and no one better off.[22] The force of the LDO derives from a principle in the vein of the following:

The Person-affecting Principle
One outcome A cannot be better or worse than another outcome B, in any relevant sense, if it is not better or worse for someone.[23]

The person-affecting principle (PAP) gives a justification of why it is problematic to violate principle 1 and 2. One could now claim that the levelling down, from A* to B*, is in no sense an improvement. It is not an improvement, since it is not better for the people in B*, given that they have the same amount of welfare as before, nor is it better for the people in A*, as they are made worse off by the levelling down. Furthermore how can B* in any relevant sense be equally as good as A, if everyone in A is better off than everyone in B*? This is the traditional LDO applied to our two cases of comparison (the one between A and B* and the one between A* and B*).

However, this way of reasoning only works if the populations A (or A*) and B* involve *necessary people*. Necessary people are people that have existed, exist or will exist independently of our choices. When we make comparative evaluations of outcomes like A (or A*) and B* it could nevertheless be the case that these outcomes did not involve necessary people, but rather *contingent people*. Contingent people are people whose existence is dependent on our choices and therefore only exist in some but not all of the possible outcomes available to us. In order to make clear the latter possibility imagine that the comparative evaluation of, say, A and B* could (borrowing from an example by Parfit) be described as follows:[24]

> *Two Different Policies*
> Let us accept that we can adopt one and only one of two policies concerning our use of resources: policy I (call it the conservation policy) or policy II (call it the depletion policy). If we adopt conservation, it will follow that in 300 years from now population A* will emerge. If, on the other hand, we adopt depletion it follows that population B* will emerge instead. Assume furthermore that the people in population A* and B* would be different people, thus having different identities.

In this scenario, as we shall see, it will follow from egalitarianism (whether monistic or pluralistic, or whether measured by the SV or the NSV) that B*, in at least one relevant sense, is better than A*. My objection to egalitarianism in cases involving different contingent people cannot, as we shall see shortly, be stated in terms of the traditional levelling down objection.

In cases involving contingent people, adherents of the traditional levelling down objection *cannot* argue against egalitarianism as they used to do.

Firstly, *no one* is worse off if population B* is brought into existence because of the depletion policy. If B* is brought into existence, population A* will not exist and therefore cannot be worse off in any relevant sense. And the people in B* are not worse off (compared to non-existence) since they have lives worth living. Secondly, some are better off if population B* is brought into existence; the people in B* are better off by being brought into existence compared to non-existence! At least, this is a plausible kind of reasoning if we believe that existence can, instrumentally, benefit a person. And why should we not do so, given that most of us believe that bringing a person into existence, who will, for instance, always suffer from extreme pain, can harm such a person? So, if being brought into existence can harm a person, then being brought into existence can also benefit her – if she experiences a good life – thus making her better off than no life at all. It will thus be better for the people in B* to exist than not to exist.[25]

So in one relevant sense B* is better than A*, namely for the B*-people. In what follows A* and B* will represent different contingent people.

However, it seems correct to say the following: If you are a monistic egalitarian, B* is better than A* – but then, as we have already seen, principle 1 is violated – and that is not acceptable. On the other hand, if you are a pluralistic egalitarian, you are not committed to violate principle 1, as the larger total sum of welfare in A* could be the additional moral factor that outweighs the surplus (of the moral factor) of equality in B*. However, in cases involving different contingent people both monistic- and pluralistic egalitarianism, as we have seen in the case with necessary people, also violate principle 2. But, as we have just see, this violation is unproblematic, since B* is better than A* in one relevant sense.

A final comment, just mentioned as an idea for those egalitarians who are reluctant to embrace the person-affecting principle.[26] One could argue that egalitarianism, in the evaluation of outcomes that represents different contingent people, is still the proper target of a kind of levelling down. However, it is a levelling down that is different from the traditional levelling down. The kind of levelling down that I have in mind is a kind of levelling down which does not imply that someone is *the subject* of levelling down and therefore is made worse off than before. On the contrary, as we have just seen, if population B* is brought into existence (as a matter of our choice) some (the B*-people) are better off. But it is a kind of levelling down (let us call it the Impersonal Levelling Down Objection) that allows egalitarians to accept that it, at least in one sense, is better to actualise population B* instead of population A*. It is a levelling down because egalitarians accepts that a future world where all people are at a lower welfare level is better, at least concerning equality, than a future world where everybody has much better lives, though that future world will not be perfectly equal.

In sum, my objection is that egalitarianism is not always subject to the traditional levelling down objection, but rather, when it comes to choices that involve different contingent people, to an Impersonal Levelling Down Objection.

(iv) CONCLUSION

I hope to have shown that some versions of egalitarianism entail the RC or conclusions that are like the RC. Thus, it is not just total utilitarianism that needs to answer the objection raised by the RC. The scope of the objection should also cover the discussed versions of egalitarianism. Furthermore, I have argued that these versions of egalitarianism imply conclusions that are otherwise repugnant. These latter repugnant conclusions draw on the plausibility of principle 1 and 2, but could also be supported by the levelling down objection.

But, as I have also tried to argue, the levelling down objection, in its traditional form, has no force in cases involving the evaluation of outcomes containing contingent people. Instead, egalitarianism is in these cases subject to an impersonal levelling down objection.

Notes

1. Thanks to Nils Holtug and Wlodek Rabinowicz for valuable comments on an earlier version of this paper. Thanks also to the participants at the workshop on Ethical Theory and Meta-ethics at Roskilde University (Denmark) on December 9th 2003, where I had the opportunity to discuss the main ideas of this paper.
2. Parfit 1984, p. 388. I have added the parentheses.
3. For philosophers who use the term 'total utilitarianism' see e.g. Temkin 1993, and Holtug 1999.
4. Total utilitarianism is usually opposed to *average utilitarianism* which, besides the consequentialist component, accepts that 'the best outcome is the one with the greatest average sum of welfare value', see e.g. Smart & Williams 1973 pp. 27-28. For a critique of average utilitarianism see e.g. Kagan 1998 pp. 46-47.
5. Cf. Glover 1977, p. 69-71, Munthe 1996 p. 29, Tännsjö 1992 og 2002, Ryberg 1996, p. 134-165, Kymlicka 2002, p. 33-37.
6. Some have discussed the RC as an objection to The Priority View. See e.g. Holtug 1999 and Petersen 2002.
7. Many people have posed the LDO against egalitarianism. See e.g. Raz 1986, p. 240, Parfit 1998, p. 9-10, Holtug 1998.
8. Kagan 1998, p. 49.
9. Within distributive egalitarianism there exists a vast amount of more specific theories that turn on answers to the question of what kinds of inequalities that are morally unjust. Are, for instance, inequalities that are the result of peoples' own choices morally unjust and should they thus be subsidised? See e.g. Scheffler 2003, Vallentyne 2002, or Lippert-Rasmussen 2001 for discussions of such questions.
10. In what follows I will write 'equality' instead of the longer 'equality (or inequality)'.

11. For an example of how differently one can measure equality/inequality within the SV, see Temkin 1993, chapter 5.
12. In this comparison of outcomes we need not differentiate between whether equality is measured by the SV or the NSV, as monistic egalitarianism will deliver the same answer no matter which of the two measurements of equality is brought into play. By the way, the last sentence has been added for stylistic reasons in order to formulate some repugnant conclusions that in form resemble the original RC.
13. This will be true no matter what kind of standard of measurement (whether the SV or the NSV) is employed.
14. This principle is modelled on a Pareto principle which says: 'A distribution is optimal if and only if there is no feasible alternative distribution in which at least one person is better off and no one is worse off'. For adherents of this principle see e.g. Ng 1980, p. 31 and Griffin 1986, p. 147. For critics see e.g. Cohen 1995 and Shaw 1999.
15. For an excellent description of the difference between necessary and contingent people see Bykvist 1998 chapter 5.
16. Repugnant conclusions that would violate the following principles could easily be constructed, as in the discussion of monistic egalitarianism in section (ii) a. However, for brevity I have omitted an explicit description of them in the text.
17. This principle cannot be derived from the Pareto Principle, as it does not entail the clause 'in any relevant sense'.
18. For adherents of the view that equality has positive value in itself, see e.g. Temkin 1993. See Persson 2001 for the view that unjust inequality is intrinsically bad, whereas equality has neutral value.
19. While this strategy clearly works in the comparative evaluation between A and B*, it does not necessarily work in the comparison between A* and B*. However, it could work in the latter comparison, if the equality relations that exist in A* (apart from the one person) at a higher level weigh more heavily than the larger amount of equality relations at the lower level of B*.
20. I do not know of anyone who has developed this strategy in detail, but Kasper Lippert-Rasmussen made me aware of the possibility.
21. Many people have posed the LDO against egalitarianism. See note 6 in this paper.
22. See Temkin 1993 and Persson 2001 for a critique of the LDO.
23. For a wording of the person-affecting principle very much like this see Temkin 1993, pp. 249-55, Heyd 1992, pp. xi-xii and Roberts 1998, p. 1.
24. I here follow Parfit's example in Parfit 1984, pp. 361-64.
25. See e.g. Holtug 2001 for a convincing argument that it is valuable for individual P to come into existence, if P has a life worth living. See also Petersen 2001 for a critique of the view that individuals cannot benefit from coming into existence.
26. See, for instance, Temkin 1993.

References

Bykvist, Krister (1998) *Changing Preferences: A Study in Preferentialism*, Dissertation (Uppsala University).

Glover, Jonathan (1977) *Causing Death and Saving Lives* (Penguin Books).

Cohen, Gerald Allan (1995) The Pareto Argument for Inequality, *Social Philosophy and Policy*, Vol. 12, pp.160-185.

Griffin, James (1986) *Well-Being. Its Meaning, Measurement and Moral Importance* (Oxford, Clarendon Press).

Heyd, David (1992) *Genethics* (University of California Press).
Holtug, Nils (1998) Egalitarianism and the levelling down objection, *Analysis*, Vol. 58 (2), pp. 166-174.
Holtug, Nils (1999) Utility, Priority and Possible People, *Utilitas* Vol. 11, No. 34, pp. 16-36.
Holtug, Nils (2001) On the Value of coming into Existence, *Journal of Ethics*, Vol 3 (4), pp. 361-384.
Holtug, Nils (forthcoming)
Kagan, Shelly (1998) *Normative Ethics* (Westview Press).
Kymlica Will (2002) *Contemporary Political Philosophy*, second edition, (Oxford University Press).
Lippert-Rasmussen, Kasper (2001) Equality, Option Luck and Responsibility, *Ethics,* Vol. 111, pp. 548-579.
Munthe, Christian (1996) The Argument From Transfer, *Bioethics*, Vol. 10, pp. 27-42.
Ng, Yew Kwang (1980) *Welfare Economics: The Introduction and Development of Basic Concepts* (New York: Wiley)
Parfit, Derek (1984) *Reasons and Persons* (Oxford University Press).
Parfit, Derek (1986) Overpopulation and the Quality of Life, in Singer P. (Ed.) *Applied Ethics* (Oxford University Press).
Parfit, Derek (1998) Equality and Priority, in Mason A. (Ed.) *Ideals of Equality* (Oxford, Blackwell)
Persson, Ingmar (2001) Equality, Priority and Person-affecting value, *Ethical Theory and Moral Practice*, Vol. 4, pp. 23-39.
Petersen, Thomas S. (2001) Generocentrism, *Philosophia, Philosophical Quarterly of Israel*, Vol. 1-4, pp. 411-423.
Petersen, Thomas S. (2002) The Claim From Adoption, *Bioethics*, Vol.16, No. 4, pp. 353-375.
Portmore, Douglas. (1999) Does the Total Principle Have any Repugnant Implications? *Ratio* Vol. 12:1., pp. 80-98.
Raz, Joseph (1986) *The Morality of Freedom* (Oxford Clarendon Press)
Roberts, Melinda A. (1998) *Child versus Childmaker* (Rowman & Littlefield Publishers, Inc.).
Ryberg, Jesper (1996) Is the Repugnant Conclusion Repugnant?, *Philosophical Papers* XXV, pp. 161-177.
Scheffler, Samuel (2003) What is Egalitarianism? *Philosophy and Public Affairs*, Vol.31:1, pp. 5-39.
Shaw, Patrick (1999) The Pareto Argument and Inequality, *The Philosophical Quarterly*, Vol. 49, No. 196, pp. 354-368.
Smart, J.J.C. & Williams Bernard (1973) *Utilitarianism for and against* (Cambridge University Press).
Tännsjö, Törbjörn (1992) Who are the Beneficiaries?, *Bioethics,* Vol. 6, pp. 288-296.
Tännsjö, Törbjörn (1998) *Hedonistic Utilitarianism* (Edinburgh Press).
Tännsjö, Törbjörn (2002) Why We Ought to Accept the Repugnant Conclusion, *Utilitas* vol. 14, No. 3. November pp. 339-359.
Temkin, Larry (1993) *Inequality* (Oxford University Press).
Vallentyne, Peter (2002) Brute Luck, Option Luck, and Equality of Opportunities, *Ethics,* Vol. 112, pp. 529-557.